Perhaps one of the best known an
of the Old Testament, *Jonah* gives u
the grace of God in the gospel especialy as it impacts a pharisaical
heart. Colin Smith is a faithful guide in helping us come to terms
with Jonah's message for the church today.

Liam Goligher
Senior Minister, Tenth Presbyterian Church, Philadelphia, Pennsylvania

Here is a pastor reading the book of Jonah and finding a preacher who
wants settled ministry, not challenges; who wants to see his enemies
crushed, not converted; who longs for God's grace in his own life,
but not in the lives of others; who knows how to speak God's words
with faithfulness, but who wants to see only the component of
judgment worked out in reality; a preacher who is angry and who
wants God to be angry too; a man who wallows in self-pity and
hates it when God exposes that self-pity for the idolatrous arrogance
it is. It is not difficult to see the relevance of such portraits in our
own day. And what does it say of God, that he keeps working away
at Jonah as he keeps working away at the Ninevites?

D. A. Carson
Research Professor of New Testament,
Trinity Evangelical Divinity School, Deerfield, Illinois

This outstanding book not only presents the exciting story of Jonah
interestingly, it also applies the story so that God can speak into our
personal lives through it. It can be consulted with great profit by anyone
preparing a talk or discussion from Jonah. I also recommend it as
a devotional book that can be read for inspiration and edification.

Ajith Fernando
Teaching Director, Youth for Christ, Sri Lanka

This is a heart-searching and Christ-proclaiming book written from
a pastor's heart. With careful observation and penetrating application,
Colin Smith opens up the book of Jonah showing it to be both a mirror
and a window. As a mirror it exposes our innate self-centredness. As
a window it reveals the heart of God seen most clearly in the grace,
patience and compassion of the Lord Jesus. Do not read this book if you
want to stay the same. Expect to be humbled, convicted, challenged,

comforted and changed. The heart-warming, inescapable conclusion is that salvation truly comes from the Lord.

Jonathan Prime
Pastor, Enfield Evangelical Free Church, Enfield, England

If you want a concise book about a much misunderstood prophet then you have found it here. Colin Smith is a master at unlocking the Bible, he provides us with accessible and reliable theology along with so many bridges of practical and judicious application to the contemporary Church and society. The strength of the book is that it echoes the ministry of a prophet, speaking God's words into a culture which resists that word. *Jonah: Navigating a God-centred Life* is a model of that much maligned and ill-used concept, relevance. He speaks of Jonah's 'prophetic scoop' and his subsequent struggles with his own ego and with God's demands on his life.

It's amazing how many hot potatoes are tackled head on. Colin is so helpful on, the purpose of trouble, struggles with guidance, prayer, election and self-absorption. You will meet Jesus on the pages of Jonah, 'Christ endured the worm and the wind so that you could be brought into an eternity under God's vine.'

You will be blown away by some great illustrations. Look out for the one on the savior, the monk and the beggar. You will also have to agree with me that the Super Bowl parking story must be up in the ten best illustrations ever!

After reading this book your prayer will be, 'Lord, make me less like Jonah and more like Jesus.'

David C Meredith
Senior Minister, Smithton-Culloden Free Church, Inverness, Scotland

No matter how well you think you know the story of Jonah, you will be blessed and enlightened by this book from a gifted pastor who has both a good grasp of Scripture and human nature. In these pages we see ourselves, running from God but always brought back by God's intervention and grace. In this helpful exposition we will recognize the same providence and patience of God in our lives as Jonah experienced. Read this book and share it with a friend.

Erwin Lutzer
Senior Pastor, The Moody Church, Chicago

Jonah:

Navigating a God-centered Life

Colin S. Smith

CHRISTIAN
FOCUS

Colin Smith is Senior Pastor of The Orchard Evangelical Free Church in the northwest suburbs of Chicago. Born and raised in Edinburgh, Scotland he trained at the London School of Theology where he earned the degrees of Bachelor of Theology and Master of Philosophy. Before coming to the states in 1996, Colin served as Senior Pastor of the Enfield Evangelical Free Church in London.

He is the author of eight books including, *Unlocking the Bible Story* and *10 Keys for Unlocking the Bible*. His preaching ministry is shared through the daily radio program, 'Unlocking the Bible' and through his website, UnlockingtheBible.org.

Unless otherwise stated, Scripture quotations taken from *The Holy Bible, New International Version*. Copyright © 1973, 1978, 1984 by Biblica. Used by permission.

Scripture quotations marked "KJV" are taken from the King James Version.

A CIP catalogue record for this book is available from the British Library.

ISBN 1-84550-639-1

10 9 8 7 6 5 4 3 2

First published in 2012
by
Christian Focus Publications,
Geanies House, Fearn, Ross-shire,
IV20 1TW, Scotland, UK
www.christianfocus.com

Cover design by Daniel Van Straaten

Printed by Bell & Bain, Glasgow

MIX
Paper from
responsible sources
FSC® C007785

Contents

For Emily and Katie

May you find great joy in pursuing
God-centered lives

••

Introduction

This book is about the disturbing possibility that, having pledged your life to Christ, you may end up spending much of that life avoiding the God you set out to serve. It's about the conflict in the heart of every Christian and the grace of God that, when you see it, will draw you into the pursuit of a God-centered life.

God-centered lives are driven by a passion for His Son Jesus Christ that shows itself in love, trust and obedience towards Him. You can't define this life with a list of activities because the ventures to which it may lead are too many to describe. So this book is not about what you are doing, but about what drives you in what you are doing.

Our journey will take us beyond the predictable discussion of the disciplines of a God-centered life, such as praying, reading, serving, giving, loving, trusting, persevering, worshiping and witnessing. You already know that you need to do these things, but how are you to pursue them? How can you navigate a God-centered life?

I assume from the fact that you are reading this book that you are a Christian, that you are dissatisfied with the shallow brands of Christianity that pander to your comfort and convenience, and that God has already planted a desire in your heart to break free from the bonds of self interest and to pursue Him with a holy passion.

Also I assume that you have discovered the strange contradiction that lies at the heart of all Christian experience: while loving Christ, you find yourself turning from Him; while trusting Christ you often battle with fear and anxiety; while serving Christ, you sometimes struggle with disappointment, and wonder about the events that have unfolded in your life.

You are not alone.

What's going on inside me?

Christians are a mass of contradictions. We are righteous in Christ, and yet we sin every day. We have the power of the Spirit, and yet we feel our own weakness. Christ's work in us has begun, but it is not yet complete.

When Christ invaded your life, He opened your mind, changed your heart and moved your will in a new direction. The Bible calls this 'regeneration' or the new birth. It is a miracle in which the person you were died and a new creation was brought into being.

Being crucified and buried with Christ, you have been raised to a new life in Him, and the first signs of this new life are that you believe in Christ, confess Him as Lord and Savior, and offer yourself to Him. With this new life, you have a new capacity. God's Spirit lives in you, giving you power and desire to pursue a God-centered life, that otherwise would be beyond both your ability and your interest.

All of this is true of you in Christ. If it was the whole truth the Christian life would be easy. But it's not.

Your new life of faith is lived out in the body (Gal. 2:20). This means that your flesh—the remnants of the person you were before Christ took control of your life—will always be throwing up new opportunities and enticements to sin, with which you have to deal. The Holy Spirit draws you toward adventurous faith and costly obedience, but the flesh says, "No!" always.

As I write, a major oil company has just sealed an oil well that has been pumping millions of gallons of oil into the Gulf of Mexico. Teams of engineers have battled for weeks to cap the well head, but the depth from which the oil comes, the force with which it erupts, and the sheer volume released has stretched the ingenuity of the engineers to the limit.

The oil well is a helpful picture of the flesh which is an endless source of pollution and corruption in your life. Sin inhabits the deep places of the Christian heart. James was writing to believers when he said that "each one is tempted when, by his own evil desire, he is dragged away and enticed" (James 1:14).

The source of sin lies closer to home than you or I may want to admit. It's easy to blame God or the devil for our struggles, but the primary source of our sin lies within our own hearts. Explaining temptation by saying "God is testing me" or "Satan is attacking me" positions "me" either as the victim, if I am defeated, or the hero, if I prevail. But confessing that "My heart is desperately wicked" provides no such comforts. It heads off all attempts to shift blame, and cuts down all the pretensions of spiritual pride.

Sin remains in the hearts of even the most mature believers, and it is never passive. Sin shows itself in dark moods, powerful temptations, selfish ambition, callous words, coldness of heart, and anger with God—to name just a few examples. Like the renegade oil well, your flesh is always forcing some new polluting thoughts or desires to the surface of your life. This dark and toxic mixture, hidden in your heart, keeps breaking through the sea floor of your life in new and unexpected ways. In this life, you will always battle with the 'well' of your flesh.

At our best, Christians are always Christian sinners, who depend wholly on the righteousness of Jesus Christ, counted as ours, in our union with Him through the bond of faith. If God were to judge believers on our performance in the Christian life, none of us would make it to heaven.

You will depend on the righteousness of Christ, counted as yours as much on the day you enter heaven as you did on the day you first trusted Christ. However far you grow in godliness, you will never be able to stake your claim before God on the quality of your obedience. You hang on the life Christ lived for you because you daren't stand on the life you have lived for Him.

A map for the journey

We're going to explore the complex inner life of a Christian by following the story of Jonah, a mature believer widely known and respected for his public ministry, who became absorbed with himself and in large measure failed to live a God-centered life.

God spoke through Jonah and his preaching changed people's lives. But behind this man's celebrated ministry lay an intense private battle as the deep wells of selfish desire, love of comfort, and resentment towards God erupted repeatedly in his life.

The outline of Jonah's story is simple. God called this man out of a settled ministry in Israel to preach in Nineveh, a city notorious for its wickedness. Jonah didn't like the idea, so he got on a ship and sailed in the opposite direction. God intercepted the ship by sending a storm and when the crew realized that the storm had come because of Jonah, they threw him overboard.

God rescued Jonah by providing a great fish that swallowed him, swam to the shore, and then spat him up on the beach. At this point, Jonah decided he had better do what God said, so he went to Nineveh and preached the message God had given. When the people heard Jonah, they believed God, repented of their sin and were saved from immanent judgment.

You might think that a man who experienced miracles in his own life, and whose ministry was used by God to transform one of the most violent cities of his time, would get beyond the struggles that 'ordinary' Christians experience. But Jonah shows us something different. At the end of the book, after the miracle of being saved by the fish and after seeing a whole city repent, Jonah was angry, dissatisfied and out of sorts with God. Instead of rejoicing, he slumped into despair, and became convinced that his life had no further meaning or value.

Jonah's story begins with him running from God and ends with him arguing against God, which raises the interesting question of when his book was written. You can't write under the inspiration of the Holy Spirit when you are arguing with God, so I assume that Jonah wrote this book late in his life and that his account offers his mature reflection on the triumph of God's grace.

Some people teach us by their example; Jonah teaches us by his confession. His widely appreciated ministry was a thin veneer over his continuing self-interest, and through a large part of his life, he avoided the God he professed to serve.

A mirror and a window

Jonah's confession is like a mirror in which you will see the struggles and enigmas of your own inner life. This man was a prophet, a mature believer who had given his life to a widely appreciated ministry in which He spoke the word of God with clarity and power, but still he struggled with the impulses of his own self-interest. That tells you something important. Pursuing a God-centered life won't make your struggles easier; it will make them harder.

This may seem like a strange enigma, but those who throw themselves most fully into God's service often experience inner conflict most intensely. So it's important to know that pursuing a God-centered life will intensify your battle. You will be swimming against the tide and that means that your struggles will increase. As you become more useful to Christ you will find yourself in the heat of a spiritual battle. Jonah experienced this and his candid confession maps the battle for us as we set out to navigate a God-centered life.

As we journey through this story you will also discover a window into the heart of God, who is the hero of Jonah's story. God has the first word, calling Jonah to a new ministry and unsettling his comfortable life. And

God has the last word, confronting Jonah's self-indulgence and revealing the extent of His own compassion. Then at the center of the story, Jonah compresses all that he has learned into a single sentence: "Salvation comes from the LORD" (Jonah 2:9).

Through his honest confession of failure, Jonah wants us to know what he discovered about the grace of God. Jonah's story is full of God's redeeming love, His extraordinary patience, and His relentless pursuit of lost people. The story could only have been written by a man who, being humbled by his own failure, found that he could rejoice in God's ultimate triumph.

If you work long and hard in the cause of Christ, there may be times when you feel that God cares about what you are doing more than He cares about you. It isn't so. If God cared only about getting His work done, He would have ditched Jonah and sent someone else to Nineveh. If the work was all that mattered, God could have abandoned Jonah in the self-indulgent resentment that gripped him after the people of Nineveh had repented. But God cared about Jonah, and God cares about you more than you can imagine.

God saved a vast city from judgment through Jonah's ministry, but the salvation of the city gets very little attention in the book. The big story is about God's patience and perseverance with one struggling believer. God went to extraordinary lengths to rescue one man from the power of his rebellious will and the self-interest of his despondent heart. That gives me hope. Jonah's story opens a window into the heart of God where you will discover His faithful, persevering and ultimately triumphant love.

By any standards Jonah lived an extraordinary life. Few have the privilege of preaching with such power that a whole city is transformed, and nobody I know has experienced God's grace through being swallowed by a fish! But despite Jonah's uniqueness, his story speaks to our more ordinary lives in powerful ways.

Jonah's confession maps out our battle and gives testimony to the patience, perseverance and ultimate triumph of God's grace in the conflicted experience of a Christian believer. Our journey with Jonah will help you to explore the dynamics of your own struggle with God. It will challenge your self-interest, and give you a fresh glimpse of God's invincible grace. May God use this book to show you His hand in the storms you experience and to help you navigate a God-centered life.

1

Embrace God's Call

God has a way of disturbing our dreams. We plan our families, our finances, our ministries and our futures. Then God breaks into the plan, and suddenly life is set on a different course. A child is born, a loved one dies, an accident happens, an illness is diagnosed, a disaster hits, the stock market collapses, you lose your job, your son rebels, your church divides; your life is torn apart.

When God interrupts your life, He is calling you to follow Him in a new way. By breaking into your settled pattern, He is moving you to a new place where you can make fresh discoveries of His grace. Embracing God's call is never easy, but this is where the pursuit of a God-centered life begins, and where the shame of a self-centered life is exposed.

Jonah had no idea of how self-absorbed he had become until God disturbed his comfortable life. He was devoted to ministry and listened, as a prophet, to the voice of God. But while he was ministering to others, his own heart had grown cold and, when God called Jonah to something new, the hidden layers of his inner life were revealed.

Jonah enjoyed a comfortable life until God interrupted his dream. Born in a godly home, and raised with knowledge of the truth, he quickly developed a love for God and a heart for ministry. People in his hometown of Gath Hepher enjoyed Jonah's preaching and, with his obvious gift as an effective communicator, he soon established a fine reputation as a much loved and deeply respected teacher of God's Word.

Early in his ministry, God gave Jonah a prophetic scoop that established his ministry. Jonah announced that the borders of Israel would be extended during the reign of King Jeroboam and when this happened, his reputation was made. He was hailed as God's "servant Jonah ... *the* prophet from Gath Hepher," as if there wasn't another prophet worthy of the name (from 2 Kings 14:25).*

Serving in Gath Hepher, Jonah enjoyed the luxury of a loyal and responsive audience. Godly people wanted to hear His Word in those days just as they do today, and so Jonah would have been in big demand. If he was in ministry today, Jonah would have a full schedule of speaking engagements, his books would be best sellers, and his page on Facebook would be bombarded by fans. Jonah enjoyed a good life doing good work in a good place. He was living his dream until, one day, God interrupted his life.

A dream interrupted

> *The word of the LORD came to Jonah son of Amittai: "Go to the great city of Nineveh and preach against it, because its wickedness has come up before me." (Jonah 1:1-2)*

---

* Throughout, italics in quotations from Scripture mark my emphasis.

Put yourself in Jonah's shoes and try to imagine what this interruption was like. You are enjoying a successful ministry among God's people. You are well known and well appreciated for your celebrated prophecy about restoring the borders of Israel. You feel settled, fulfilled and contented, but now the Word of God disturbs your comfortable 'Christian' life.

God is calling you to leave the people you love, move to a new location and venture into an uncertain future. Your assignment is to serve people of another race, who regard you as an enemy, and you are to do this by speaking 'against' the great city of Nineveh. Instead of prophesying blessing on God's people, your new calling is to pronounce judgment on God's enemies. Nothing in this new calling is attractive to you. It all seems like an overwhelming loss.

The Word of God came to this successful prophet with a settled ministry and, when it did, the music stopped in Jonah's life. I expect that Jonah was caught up in the relentless demands and opportunities of his ministry in Gath Hepher, but activity is a poor substitute for obedience, and God's call revealed how far he was from living a God-centered life.

If you enjoy what God has given you now, you will not find it easy when He calls you to something new. The more comfortable you are, the harder it will be. I love the work God has given me to do and so I find it really hard to keep my heart in a place where I can honestly say to the Lord, "If there's something else you want me to do, I'm willing to do it." But without that spirit, a job, a home or even a ministry can easily become an idol.

When God interrupts your life, He breaks the idol. Nothing that He gives you in this world is yours forever. Your entire life is "a mist that appears for a little while and then vanishes" (James 4:14). The home that you live in is yours for a time. The work that you do is yours for a time. The people you love are yours for a time. One day, others will live in your home, and others will continue your work. One day, others will have your money and your possessions; the opportunities now entrusted to you will be given to them.

Loving my work as I do, it's good for me to remember that, one day, someone else will sit in 'my' office. Their books will be on 'my' shelves, and their stamp will be on the ministry that is so precious to me. I need to hold what God has given lightly. It will not be forever. The person who learns to number his or her days gains a heart of wisdom (Ps. 90:12).

The fear of something new

In over thirty years as a pastor, I have only moved once. That was after sixteen years of serving a wonderful congregation in Enfield, North London. Saying goodbye wasn't easy, but we were helped by anticipating the joy of serving a new congregation in the suburbs of Chicago. Jonah had no such comfort. Losing the work that he loved was compounded by the fearsome prospect of his new calling: to preach judgment to the enemies of God.

In Jonah's day, one dark superpower cast a shadow over all the surrounding nations. The Assyrians were known for their brutality. They had refined the art of torture in ways that would make you wish you hadn't read of them, so I'll spare you the details. It's enough to know that the Assyrians were the terror of Jonah's time.

Nineveh was the decadent and violent center of the Assyrian empire. The prophet Nahum describes it as "the city of blood, full of lies, full of plunder, never without victims" (Nahum 3:1). Not exactly the kind of place you would choose for a vacation. How would you feel if God called you to serve Him in a land known for terror and torture?

For Jonah to move from a ministry of pronouncing blessing on God's friends to the work of pronouncing judgment on God's enemies would mean embracing an unrecognizably different life and it is hardly surprising that he balked at the prospect of what God was calling him to endure.

I've tried to imagine Jonah's interaction with God:

"Jonah, I want you to go …"
"Lord I am really happy with what I am doing for You here."
"I want you to do something else."
"You want me to leave the work I love?"
"That's right."
"Where do you want me to go?"
"Nineveh."
"That's in enemy territory. There are terrorists and torturers there. What do you want me to say?"
"Preach against the city, because its wickedness has come up before me."

It's hardly surprising that Nineveh's wickedness had come up before God. It was certainly before the eyes of God's people. Many in Israel would have prayed for Assyria to be overthrown, just as Christians today might pray for the demise of nations that pose a threat to our way of life. If God had destroyed Nineveh as He destroyed Sodom and Gomorrah, it would have brought great relief and joy to Israel and to the surrounding nations. But God loved the Assyrian people. He saw their wickedness, and yet even when it came up before Him, He had compassion on them and reached out to them, by sending Jonah.

Nothing is more disturbing to a comfortable faith or a comfortable church than God's passion for the world. Jonah was happy serving people of his own race, but when God called him to serve people of another race, in a country hostile to his own, the selfishness of Jonah's heart was exposed. The prophet known and acclaimed for his fruitful ministry had lost touch with God's heart and God's mission in the world. Jonah was a long way from navigating a God-centered life, but no one, not even the prophet himself, would have known it until God stepped in.

How God interrupts your life

God's Word came to Jonah with such force and directness that there was no doubt in Jonah's mind that God was speaking and that God was sending him to Nineveh. Being a prophet meant that Jonah received direct revelation from God. The *Lord* spoke to him as a man speaks with his friend.

It's different for us. God speaks to us through the Scriptures, and since the Bible does not contain individual instructions on where you should live, whom you should marry, or what work you should do, God's interruptions in your life will usually come through secondary means. An interruption may come through unwelcome decisions made by other people, or through circumstances beyond your control. Something unexpected happens and your whole life is completely different. You lose the life that you love and you face a future that you fear.

So let's look at some examples of what God's interruption might look like in your life today. The characters in the following scenes are fictitious, but they represent familiar situations. We begin with a challenge close to the one faced by Jonah.

Jim and Julie's new assignment

Jim and Julie had served as missionaries for ten years. They were the first couple to join the field leaders when their mission began work in the country where they serve. Making the move half way round the world from their home in the American midwest took extraordinary courage. Learning a new language and adapting to an alien culture seemed an impossible task, but Jim and Julie persevered.

After ten years of hard work, a small but robust fellowship of local Christians had been established with about fifty believers meeting in homes for worship, teaching and encouragement. Jim and Julie were like a mother and father to these people. The church had become their life.

The previous year, the mission with whom they served adopted a policy that called for missionaries to move to a new assignment after ten years. Someone from the mission visited with Jim and Julie to talk about what this would mean for them. It was not an easy meeting.

"You don't understand," Jim said. "These believers need us here. We're not in a position to move to another town."

The man from the mission pressed his point. "These believers belong to Christ, not to you," he said. "As long as you are here, they will depend on you. They won't step up and take responsibility unless and until you move on."

"Besides," he continued, "the mission you signed up for was to reach this country, and there are other towns where new churches could be planted. You have shown great courage in leaving your home and building a new life here. Now we are asking you to leave the work you have established and bring the gospel to another community."

After the meeting Julie told Jim that she would "rather go back home than put up with being pushed about like this." She felt it was up to each missionary to decide what is best for his or her own situation, and she didn't have a good word to say about the man from the mission.

Michael's company

As his wife was pregnant with their first child, Michael made the decision that he wanted to start his own business. He had grown weary of working for people who cared more about themselves than their customers. He wanted to create his own software company, where he could glorify God with the way he and his team acted toward customers and employees in the marketplace. Michael wanted to set a godly example for his family, and felt sure that he could do this better by building his own company based on godly values than by carrying on in the frustrations of his present work. With a child on the way, Michael felt called to pursue this dream now.

Under his leadership, Michael's new company thrived. Prospective customers, talented employees, and shrewd investors were drawn to his company's fresh way of doing business. As the business grew, Michael received many accolades. Three years after the company's founding, he was named one of the top one hundred entrepreneurs in the country. Shortly thereafter, his Christian college alma mater asked him to deliver the commencement speech at its graduation ceremony on the topic of "Godly values in the world of commerce." Things were going better than he could have ever dreamed.

One day, Michael's investors called to tell him they had received an unsolicited bid to buy the company. The offer made financial sense for all of the company's stakeholders, and opened the door for Michael's company to reach new markets around the world.

The problem for Michael is that he would no longer be the CEO. The acquiring company wanted to keep him on as vice-president of product management. Instead of being the leader, Michael would have to be a follower, and Michael had got so used to his role as the unquestioned person in charge that the idea of working under the direction of someone else was making him uncomfortable.

Michael knew that the takeover made sense for his employees, for his customers and for the investors. But the change wouldn't be easy for Michael. So he began taking actions that slowed down the deal, and soon he was at the point of jeopardizing it altogether.

Michael started out with a vision of modeling godly values in which he cared for his employees and customers. But the takeover was uncovering hidden layers of self-interest in his own heart of which he had not even been aware.

Angela's daughter

Angela had raised two daughters without support from her husband, who walked out shortly after their younger daughter was born. Living in a small town, she had survived in large measure through the help of her family and friends, all of whom were deeply involved in the local church.

When her husband left, Angela determined that she would make a success of raising her family. She found a part-time job and then poured herself into providing a stable, loving and God-honoring home for Christine and Stacy.

Angela's daughters had all the advantages of a thorough grounding in truth. She taught them to memorize Scripture verses, and led family prayers at the end of their meals. The girls made good friends in the youth group, and God used them to lead other girls in their school to faith in Christ. People in the church commented on the sweetness of these girls and how their modest charm was a credit to their remarkable mother.

Angela met regularly with three other women who had covenanted together to pray for their children. These women encouraged each other in maintaining ordered and godly homes, but none of them exceeded Angela in putting their high aspirations into practice. Angela's energy astonished her friends. Her disciplines were exemplary, and her capacity to handle the bumps and bruises of life seemed greater than the other women, who were doing the same job without having to work and with the support of a loving husband.

Angela's eldest daughter, Christine, married her high school sweetheart and settled with her husband a few miles from her mother's home. They attended the church and usually came 'home' for Sunday lunch. Christine was her mother's joy and delight.

Stacy was another story. As a senior at college, she hooked up with Kamal with whom she had almost nothing in common. Hearing that Kamal was not a Christian, Angela was immediately anxious, and her anxiety was intensified as Kamal seemed reluctant to visit their home, and was largely uncommunicative when he did.

Stacy's sweetness seemed to vanish overnight, and Angela noticed that her younger daughter was becoming increasingly withdrawn. There was a tension in the home when Stacy was around, something Angela had not experienced before and did not know how to handle. As the tension descended into conflict, mother and daughter soon found it difficult to be in the same room. Then Stacy walked out and moved in with Kamal.

Angela was brokenhearted and felt that God had let her down. Why had God allowed things to go so wrong with Stacy after Angela had poured herself into honoring the Lord in the way she raised her children? It made no sense to Angela. Then, she stopped meeting with the prayer group and was rarely seen at church. Christine couldn't figure out what had happened to her mother. For years, Angela had taught the girls to honor and trust the Lord, whatever happens. But now what had happened with Stacy had eclipsed everything else for Angela.

Quitting Points

Jonah ran away from the Lord *and headed for Tarshish.*
(Jonah 1:3)

When God interrupts your life, you may find that your comfort is more important and your obedience more conditional than you thought. That's how it was with Jonah. God's call exposed a thinly-veiled selfishness beneath the surface of the prophet's life.

Recoiling from what lay in the future, and knowing that he could not hold on to the past, Jonah decided it was time to quit. God had called him to Nineveh in the east. He went to the harbor at Joppa, and found a ship bound for Tarshish in the west.

What does it mean to "run away from the Lord"? Jonah was a prophet, well-schooled in all the Scriptures that had been written at that time. He knew that God is present everywhere, and would have been familiar with David's words in the Psalms:

> *Where can I go from your Spirit?*
> *Where can I flee from your presence? ...*
> *If I settle on the far side of the sea,*
> *even there your hand will guide me,*
> *your right hand will hold me fast.*

> (Ps. 139:7, 9-10)

Jonah knew that he could never escape from God's presence, but he felt that he could avoid God's call. In boarding the ship he was resigning from the work God had given him to do. He was saying, in effect, "There are other things that I can do in life besides bringing the Word of the Lord. I'm quitting this ministry and I'm going to make a new life for myself in Tarshish."

Why Tarshish? Why not stay at home and continue what he was doing in Gath Hepher? Being a prophet meant that God spoke to Jonah directly as He had spoken to Moses. When Jonah refused the call to Nineveh, he knew that God would no longer give him these prophetic revelations. Without revelation, Jonah's ministry as a prophet in Gath Hepher or anywhere else was over.

Staying at home and crafting his own prophecies was not an option. That would have made Jonah a false prophet and, in Israel, the penalty for false prophecy was death by stoning. Staying silent in Gath Hepher wasn't an option either. If a man known for speaking the Word of God suddenly had nothing to say, it would soon be obvious to everyone that there was a problem.

If Jonah had stayed in Gath Hepher, his rebellion would soon have been exposed. So the choice was simple: obey God and go to Nineveh, or quit the ministry and begin a new life with a new identity in another place. Jonah chose the latter and decided on Tarshish.

Jonah was respected as a man who spoke God's Word and led God's people, but he placed boundaries on where he would live, what he would do and how he would serve. When God disrupted his plan, his selfish heart was exposed and he quit.

At first sight, Jonah's experience may seem light years away from yours, but when the horizon looks bleak in your work, your family or your ministry, a new life in a new place can seem like an attractive option. When you feel that you are no longer appreciated, or that your hard work is bringing little reward, the temptation to slip away from the ties and commitments that define your life will be very real. The ship to Tarshish looks attractive, but it is heading into a storm.

The boat in the harbor

He went down to Joppa, where he found a ship bound for that port.
(Jonah 1:3)

When Jonah made his decision, everything seemed to fall into place. He wanted to go to Tarshish, and when he arrived at Joppa, he found a ship bound for that port. We're not told how Jonah interpreted the waiting ship, but I guess that he saw it as confirmation that he had made the right decision.

Temptation involves a convergence of inclination and opportunity. Sometimes inclination may be present when opportunity is not. At other times there may be opportunity but not inclination. But when inclination and opportunity arrive together, temptation reaches the height of its power. In Jonah's case, inclination went looking for opportunity and found it in the form of a ship headed to Tarshish.

There will always be a ship in the harbour ready to take you in the wrong direction, so don't confuse opportunity with the will of God. Circumstances can be helpful in discerning what is right when you are walking with the Lord, but they mislead the rebellious heart. The *Lord* is your shepherd. He is the one who leads you and guides you, and if you refuse what He says to you in the Scriptures, no other guidance is reliable.

You can't trust circumstances if you are resisting God's Word, and you can't trust conscience either. When Jonah boarded the ship, he lay down and fell into a deep sleep. It is difficult to sleep when your conscience is troubled, so we must assume that Jonah had succeeded not only in disobeying God but in feeling comfortable with what he had done. His conscience was at rest and he had great peace in following the self-absorbed impulses of his heart.

In seeking to protect himself, Jonah was walking into a world of self-deception from which it is not easy to escape. His instinct for self-preservation messed up his moral compass so that he could no longer distinguish right from wrong, or good from evil. The fear of the Lord is the beginning of wisdom; losing that fear is the beginning of folly.

Placing your dream on the altar of God

When God calls you to something new He may expose a thinly-veiled selfishness at the heart of your devotion to Christ. That's what happened to Jonah. It happened to Jim and Julie in their ministry, to Michael in his business, and to Angela with her family. It could happen to you.

The pattern is always the same: You pour yourself into work, family and ministry, then something unexpected happens and you discover that the work you are doing, the family you are raising, or the ministry you are leading has become more important to you than the God you set out to serve. You fall in love with your dream, the dream becomes an idol and God brings the idol down.

Our culture says 'live your dream,' but God calls you to place your dream on His altar and to keep it there at all times. It is good to have hopes and dreams for the future, but we have no rights. There are no certainties. Any dream can become an idol and, if it does, God will bring it down. He may interrupt your life at any moment, and call you to honor Him in something you have never faced before.

When Abraham placed Isaac on the altar of God, he was modelling something that God calls all of us to do. Isaac was a cherished gift from God and Abraham's hopes and dreams for the future lay in him. By placing Isaac on the altar, Abraham demonstrated that he loved God more than the gift God had given. With or without Isaac, Abraham was committed to a God-centered life.

Some years ago I visited a young mother in our congregation who was seriously ill. Her husband and father had asked me to join them in praying that God would spare her life. I will never forget the power of her father's prayer as we knelt around the hospital bed: "Lord you know how much we love her and we ask You to give her back to us, but we promise that if You should take her, *we will not love You less.*"

Like Abraham, this father placed his dream on the altar of God, and opened his arms to receive the gift of his daughter restored or the gift of a new and painful calling to life in this world without her. God graciously gave him what he asked.

Grace in the call

When God calls you to something new, he is always up to something good. However difficult the call may be, it is one of grace and it is for your ultimate joy. If God had not interrupted Jonah's life, his legacy would have been one prophecy, recorded in a single verse of the book of Kings (2 Kings 14:25). God had a far greater purpose for Jonah than had yet been realized in the confines of his comfortable life, and despite his faithless response, God's grace prevailed in the end.

Reflecting on Jonah's trauma—the anguish of leaving the life he loved, and the terror of going to a violent city—I've been moved by the contrast between Jonah and Jesus.

Jonah was in a good place, doing good work, enjoying a good life. Then God said, "Jonah, I want you to go to another place, and do a different work for the sake of people I love; people who are facing an imminent judgment." And Jonah said, "No."

Now consider Jesus. He was in heaven, ruling the universe by the word of His power. Adored by angels, He was in the best place, doing the best work and enjoying the best life. Then the Father said, "Go to another place, where you will be utterly rejected. Live a life that will lead to torture, crucifixion and death. Do the work of becoming an atoning sacrifice for people I love, who are facing an eternal judgment." And Jesus said, "Yes!"

I'm gripped by that contrast. Thinking about it, I've been praying: "Lord, make me less like Jonah and more like Jesus. Save me from being the kind of person who cares more about my comfort, my reputation, and my success than I do about the people You are calling me to serve. Help me to keep all of my dreams on Your altar and be ready at all times to respond with faith and obedience to Your call."

If this is the cry of your heart, I encourage you to read on. As the title of this book suggests, we're going to discover *how* to navigate a God-centered life. How can you cultivate a love for Christ that will be strong enough to overcome your natural inclinations, and deep enough to motivate a life of sacrifice? That kind of love is fuelled by what Jonah ultimately discovered: a compelling vision of the weight and wonder of God's grace.

2
Receive God's Provision

He slipped his arm round her shoulder as they looked out over the thundering waters of the Niagara Falls. The moon was shining and on this perfectly romantic evening, he hugged her close and whispered in her ear, "I love you."

She looked up with doubt in her eyes. "Really?" she asked. "I sometimes wonder."

"All right," he said, "I'll prove it."

Climbing over the protective fence, he stepped to the edge of the falls. With one huge leap he threw himself over and, as he was falling into the abyss, he screamed out "I love you."

For the bemused girl this would surely be an unforgettable experience, but the fact is that the boy's action, in this fictional scenario, would not be a demonstration of love at all. It would be a demonstration of stupidity.

The affirmation that God demonstrates his love for us in the death of His Son Jesus, stands at the heart of Christianity, but for many people the connection between God's love and the death of Jesus is less than obvious. Without further explanation, it may appear like the boyfriend making a grand gesture that is without value to the one he professes to love.

The death of Jesus can only be a meaningful demonstration of God's love is if it *achieves* something for us, and that is precisely the teaching of the New Testament. God presented Jesus as a *propitiation*, through faith in His blood (Rom. 3:25). A propitiation is a sacrifice offered to placate wrath, and Jesus became our propitiation on the cross. The wrath of God was poured out on Him as He carried our sins. By becoming our sacrifice, He delivered us from the storm of God's judgment.

I've met many people who believe that Jesus died and rose, but they don't feel that God loves them. Since they claim to believe in the cross it would be easy to assume that the answer to their problem must lie elsewhere. It doesn't. You experience the love of God by grasping what Christ has *accomplished* at the cross, and by discovering why this is good news for you.

God often teaches us through pictures, and the Bible is full of stories that serve as floodlights on the cross. In this chapter we will follow the story of the ship's crew, who began the journey of a God-centered life when they found themselves facing a judgment from God and were delivered from it by the readiness of one man to lay down his life. They faced a storm and they were saved by a sacrifice. Seeing the storm and embracing the sacrifice is where you begin in navigating a God-centered life.

The God who sends storms

Then the LORD sent a great wind on the sea, and such a violent storm arose that the ship threatened to break up. (Jonah 1:4)

There's no escaping the direct, intentional action of God in the storm. He sent a great wind on the sea. Literally, Jonah tells us, God 'hurled' this wind, as if He had thrown it out from heaven with His own hand. You could hardly have a clearer or more dramatic picture of God's direct intervention.

Storms don't happen by chance. God sustains all things by His powerful word (Heb. 1:3). The wind and the waves obey Him (Mark 4:41). That means that storms, floods, landslides, volcanoes and earthquakes happen by God's decree.

Some Christians feel that they need to protect God from this kind of exposure. Like government officials anxious to protect the President from blame over things that went wrong, they prefer to speak of God 'allowing' events like storms that wreck ships or floods that devastate thousands of lives. But God did not *allow* this storm to happen. He *made* it happen, sending the wind by His command to fulfill His purpose.

When storms come in your life, you will face an important choice in what you believe. Either you will embrace the difficult doctrine that God is in control of all things, or you will slide into viewing God as a helpless observer of your plight. Some people worry about the implications of believing that God controls all things, but I would rather live with the 'problem' of a sovereign God than with the problem of a 'god' who is a helpless observer.

A 'god' who merely allows things to happen is presumably at the mercy of another power. Such a 'god' is of no help to you in a storm because he is not in a position to *do* anything! Only the God who makes things happen can intervene in human lives to change their trajectory and give them a different outcome. That's why I find such comfort and help in the sovereignty of God.

But we need to be careful here. It would be easy to jump from the observation that storms come by God's command to the conclusion that all storms are judgments from God sent on account of human sin and disobedience. That would be a big mistake. Scripture tells us about a time when the disciples of Jesus found themselves in a storm (Mark 4:35-41). Our Lord had told them to get into the boat and so, unlike Jonah who was on the sea because of his rebellion, the disciples were on the lake because of their obedience! Obeying the Lord can get you into a storm. That's what happened to the disciples, and it may happen to you.

Storms will rage in your life, and when they do, you will find yourself trying to understand why they have come. Other people will try to help you and, like Job's friends, they may offer explanations that contain a grain of truth in a silo of confusion. When that happens, take refuge under the banner that says, "we know in part" (1 Cor. 13:9). The secret things belong to the Lord, and you will never see the full picture of what God is doing in any circumstance this side of heaven.

Explaining God's purpose in a storm is a hazardous business. What we know from the story of Jonah is that even God's judgments are means of his mercy and that God meets His people in the storm. Jonah knew that God had sent the storm on account of his disobedience, but God had other plans in play as well. He was about to redeem the ship's crew. None of these men knew the first thing about God but, through the storm, they would discover

His grace and mercy, and begin their own pursuit of God-centered lives.

Calling out to your own god

All the sailors were afraid and each cried out to his own god.
(Jonah 1:5)

The ship's crew had been through storms before. They knew what they were doing, but it soon became obvious that this time they were in trouble. The storm was so violent that the ship was about to break up.

As long as the ship held together, the sailors could hope to weather the storm, but if the ship broke up, what could be done? Fear rose and, as it did, they felt the impulse that lies deep within every human heart: they cried out for help.

But who could they cry to? These men did not know the God of the Bible. They had been raised in different cultures, each with its own religion, so each of them cried out *to his own god,* and at the same time they threw the cargo into the sea to lighten the ship.

The picture of each man crying out to his own god has immense appeal today. For many, this is exactly how a mature, pluralistic community should function. Raised in different cultures, we have very different ways of expressing religion but we are all in the same boat and when the ship is in trouble, we all turn to our respective gods for help. But there is a problem with this picture. While the image of a group of men facing a common problem, each of them crying out to his own god, would make a good poster for diversity, authenticity and cooperation, the fact remains that, when all of the calling on all of these gods was done, the storm still raged.

This brings us to the heart of a huge issue in our culture today. For many people, religion or spirituality is basically a form of self-expression, in which we voice our distinctive values through stories, rituals and traditions.

Viewed through this grid, the Bible is often seen as another projection of human hopes and fears, shaped by the thoughts and experience of Moses, and developed in a more compassionate form by Jesus. On this basis the Bible ceases to be a revelation from God, and becomes instead a resource, describing the path pursued by others in the past so that we may find our way in the future.

This worldview is so pervasive that, like the air we breathe, it is impossible to escape its influence, and that is why we need to keep coming back to the Scriptures where, if we take the Bible seriously, we find a very different story. Far from being an ideal society, the picture of every man calling out to his own god is a profound tragedy, for this reason: while many gods were invoked, none of them had power to calm the raging sea.

As their boat was about to break up, only one thing mattered. Could their gods *do something* to help them? The tragic answer was "No."

'Gods' who are a projection of our own hopes and fears cannot exceed the limits of our power. By definition, they cannot save.

The silent church in a broken world

How can you sleep? Get up and call on your god!
Maybe He will take notice of us, and we will not perish. (Jonah 1:6)

The tragedy of these men calling on gods who cannot help them is made more poignant by the fact that the one man on the ship who knew the living God was asleep below the deck. Think about this: people who do not know God are desperately calling out to gods who cannot save them while the one man who knows the sovereign *Lord* who saves is sound asleep.

Let's try and get inside Jonah's skin and experience these moments with him. Your eyes open, and you see the ship's captain towering over the berth where you have fallen asleep. He grasps the lapels of your coat and drags you to your feet. "What in the world do you think you are doing? This ship is about to break up. We're all going down. Don't you have a god you can call on?"

Jonah knew the Lord, but how could he call on God for help when he was *in the act* of rebelling against Him? Locked into an unresolved conflict with the Lord, Jonah could neither pray nor prophesy. Surrounded by unbelievers who desperately needed to know the Lord, Jonah had nothing to offer. His ministry had been silenced by his secret sin.

It's worth pausing for a moment to let the world's rebuke to the church carry its weight in our hearts: "How can you sleep? Get up and call on your God!" Think about the unbelievers in your life. If you don't pray for them, who will? The world cannot pray for itself. Only the church can intercede for a lost world and, if we are asleep, no one else will do this work.

The captain did not need Jonah's help to run the ship, but he felt a need for his prayers. The world never wants believers to have their hands on the wheel of the ship but, when trouble comes, even hardened unbelievers look for our prayers. Your unbelieving friends may not be looking for you to give direction to their lives, but when they are in a storm, they will want you to pray and they will sense that something is wrong if you don't.

What strikes me from this part of the story is that Jonah did not pray even after the captain rebuked him. The storm was raging but Jonah was still locked into his unresolved conflict with God. He couldn't pray. He wouldn't pray. His resistance to God was resolute.

It's easy to assume that you can always call on God in a storm, but it isn't that simple. Secret sins against God breed secret resentments toward Him and while these remain in the soul prayer is impossible. That is why the next step in God's gracious intervention was to expose Jonah's secret.

Exposed by tumbling dice

Come, let us cast lots to find out who is responsible for this calamity. (Jonah 1:7)

The ship's crew felt sure that the storm had not come by chance. If the gods were angry, someone must be responsible. But who? They decided to cast lots—a process rather like tossing a coin or rolling dice—believing that the gods would use this means to expose the offender. The lot fell on Jonah and his secret was out. God used tumbling dice to expose the secret sin of His rebellious servant. It was a breathtaking example of the sovereignty of God.

When God exposed Jonah's sin, it was the beginning of hope for the prophet and for the crew of the ship. The Lord disciplines those He loves and so when God exposed Jonah's sin, it was a sign of his love and evidence that God would not let His servant go.

The crew peppered Jonah with questions—"What do you do? Where do you come from? What is your country?"—until, at last, Jonah told them he was running from the Lord. Not surprisingly, they wanted to know about the God from whom Jonah was running, and so he told them, "I am a Hebrew and I worship the LORD, the God of heaven, who made the sea and the land."

When Jonah's sin was exposed, his silence was broken. At last, he was able to tell the crew about the God of the Bible who is unlike any other god. He is the God of heaven and He created the earth. He rules over winds and waves, and exposes His rebellious servants. He is the God who sends storms, the God who wrecks ships, and the God who saves them too.

The raging storm now made sense to these unbelieving men. They had no difficulty in believing that there must be a God who made the sea, and if Jonah was running from this God, they need look no further for the cause of their trouble. But what should they do?

Jonah knew what had to happen if the ship's crew was to be saved:

"Pick me up and throw me into the sea ... and it will become calm" (v. 12). How did Jonah know that the sea would become calm if they threw him out of the boat? There can only be one answer to that: God told him. When Jonah's sin was exposed, God's silence was ended, and Jonah spoke as a prophet again, telling the crew what they must do to be saved. The change was immediate. The man whose witness had been silenced by his secret sin became the mouthpiece of God to a crew on the brink of disaster.

Rowing harder

Instead, the men did their best to row back to land. But they could not, for the sea grew even wilder than before. (Jonah 1:13)

The ship's crew did not want to give Jonah up, and they tried their best to row back to the shore. Their desire to spare Jonah's life seems admirable, but it was a direct contradiction to the Word of God. God had spoken through the prophet: The life of the man who spoke the Word must be given up if the crew were to be saved. But the first instinct of the crew was to refuse the sacrifice. They felt that they could get through the storm of God's judgment, and so they rowed harder.

I want you to feel the power of this picture. God has spoken through the prophet, promising deliverance from the storm of judgment to the entire crew through the sacrifice of one man who is willing to lay down his life. But these men think that they can save themselves by their own effort. They believe that they can survive the storm without the sacrifice.

The strength of this impulse to refuse the sacrifice is significant. There is a deep-seated pride in the human heart that says, "we can make it through the judgment of God." That instinct was powerfully expressed in a poem by William Ernest Henley called *Invictus*:

> *Out of the night that covers me,*
> *Black as the Pit from pole to pole,*
> *I thank whatever gods may be*
> *For my unconquerable soul. ...*

It matters not how strait the gate,
How charged with punishments the scroll,
I am the master of my fate:
*I am the captain of my soul.**

There's great courage in that, but there's also extraordinary resistance to God. "I am the captain of my soul. It doesn't matter what judgments God may have in store, I'm in charge of my fate!" That is the polar opposite of a God-centered life, and that is where the ship's crew were: "We can row through God's storm. We don't need the sacrifice."

But they could not … These four words are the turning point of their story. When the crew realized that they could not beat the storm, they turned in their desperation to what God had said through the prophet and they staked their lives on the sacrifice of Jonah.

Do you see how beautifully this points to Jesus Christ? The storm of God's judgment is stronger than you are. You do not have the ability to survive this storm by your own effort, no matter how hard you try. The storm of God's judgment will wreck you, unless you are saved by the sacrifice of Someone else.

On the cross, Jesus gave His life to deliver you from God's righteous judgment against your sin. Cast out by men and forsaken by the Father, He offered Himself as the sacrifice that would placate the wrath of God on your behalf. At its heart, the gospel is about God's storm and His sacrifice. Christ was thrown into the storm of God's judgment so that, through His sacrifice, you would be saved.

---

* W. E. Henley (1849–1903). Found at http://en.wikipedia.org/wiki/Invictus

Our guilt in the sacrifice

Then they cried to the LORD, "O LORD, please do not let us die for taking this man's life." (Jonah 1:14)

When the ship's crew saw that the religion they had been pursuing was worthless, they abandoned their gods, and even though they had known nothing about the God of the Bible, they realized that finding peace with Him was the one thing that mattered.

The crew recognized the value of human life, so they cried to the Lord for mercy: "Do not hold us accountable for killing an innocent man, for you, O LORD, have done as you pleased" (Jonah 1:14). Jonah was innocent with regard to the crew. He had done them no wrong and they had no reason for taking his life.

Why didn't Jonah throw himself overboard and save the crew from this anxiety? The great events of the Bible story were shaped by God to throw light on what we most need to understand about our Lord Jesus Christ. Jesus did not take His own life. He was crucified, and that truth is pictured in the crew throwing Jonah overboard.

As they were guilty of sin in throwing a man who had done them no wrong overboard, so we, as members of the human race, are guilty of sin in the crucifixion of the Son of God. Yet the death in which we incur this guilt is, in God's amazing grace, the means of our salvation!

Staking your life on Jesus Christ

They took Jonah and threw him overboard, and the raging sea grew calm. (Jonah 1:15)

The ship's crew saw that they would incur guilt *in* the sacrifice as they threw Jonah overboard, and yet to their amazement they found salvation *through* the sacrifice. God's storm ended when Jonah was thrown overboard. As he was sacrificed, the ship's crew was saved.

All of this shines a light on *how* the death of Christ is a demonstration of God's love for us. We crucified the Son of God—that's our guilt in the sacrifice. Yet He chose to lay down his life for us—that is our salvation through the sacrifice.

There is, of course, this obvious and very great difference between Jonah and Jesus: Jonah was thrown into the sea on account of his own sins; Jesus was nailed to the cross on account of your sins and mine. He had no sins of His own and therefore was uniquely in a position to offer Himself as the sacrifice for our sins.

Bearing your sin and enduring your punishment, Christ was stretched out on a pole, suspended between heaven and earth and rejected by both. Christ went into the eye of the storm and offered Himself as the sacrifice absorbing the judgment of God. He endured all that hell is on the cross, so that you would never know what hell is like.

Receiving God's provision for you through the sacrifice of Jesus Christ is the first step in navigating a God-centered life. As long as you feel that there is something you can do to save yourself you will find ways to avoid giving yourself completely to the Lord. But as you see the wonder of Christ offering Himself as your propitiation, you will begin to feel that this Savior is worthy of the full devotion of your life.

Knowing that God had saved them from the storm, the crew must have felt as if they had come back from the dead and been given a whole new life. The only thing they could do was to give this life back to the God who saved them and so, feeling that they were no longer their own, they pledged their redeemed lives to God (Jonah 1:16).

Energizing a God-centered life

What would move you out of your comfort zone and energize *you* in the pursuit of a God-centered life? What would sustain *you* in faith through the disappointments and traumas of life? What would motivate *you* to bear witness to Christ in a hostile environment?

To pose the question more broadly: What will move the church out of the shallow waters of self-interest to pursue a costly ministry for the advance of Christ's kingdom around the world?

The answer to these questions came home to me with great power in the most unlikely setting. I was taking a course in church history, in which we were studying the Worldwide Missionary Conference held in my home city of Edinburgh in 1910. It was a massive ecumenical venture, one of the most comprehensive attempts to ignite a fresh passion for world mission in the entire history of the church.

The extent of the effort can be seen from the papers that fill 33 boxes, taking up 15.5 linear feet of shelf space in the archives of the Union Theological Seminary in New York. The papers include questionnaires, missionary responses from the field, transcripts, correspondence, area reports, reports to commissions, minutes, published findings and administrative records of area conferences and continuation committees.

Ploughing through the history of this massive effort to engage the church with the needs of the world, it became obvious to me that nothing much had been accomplished beyond the committees, papers and reports. This extraordinary effort made very little difference. It was a massive disappointment. But if all this effort couldn't make a difference, what would? That question haunted me.

In the providence of God, I happened at the same time to be reading a book by James Denney and discovered a message that he gave at the annual meeting of the Baptist Missionary Society, one year after the Edinburgh conference.

The aim of a keynote address at such an occasion is motivation, and the message often revolves around three well-worn themes: Pray! Give! Go! So I wish I could have been in the room when Denney announced the title for his address. It was one word: 'Propitiation.'

Denney began as follows,

Within the last twelve months, foreign missions have been more talked about in the Church than at any time I can remember. The appeals made in connection with them have been frequent and importunate. The cause has been pleaded with every kind of argument. ...

He continued,

The urgency of the need and the vastness of the opportunity have alike been pressed on the Church, and we have not wanted those who, in view of both, have talked to us of missions as a 'business proposition,' and have told us how, as men of business, we must address ourselves to the organizing and financing of the business ...

Then he asked, "What has been the result?"

As far as I can see, it is neither here nor there. An immense proportion of the people in our churches care little about the matter. There is no sensible increase either of contributions or of gifted men.

Then he came to his point:

> *It is not interest in missions that we want in our churches at this moment, but interest in the Gospel. Apart from a new interest in the Gospel, a revival of evangelical faith in Christ as the Redeemer, I believe we shall look in vain for a response to missionary appeals.*

> *But there is something in the Gospel itself ... which immediately creates missionary interest, because it has no proper correlative but the universe.*

Then, he opened up his text:

> *He (Christ) is the* propitiation *for our sins, and not for ours only, but also for the whole world* (1 John 2:2, KJV).*

Denney's point was simple: When your heart is gripped by the love of God poured out in the cross, and when you see the extent of that love in the propitiation by which Christ became *the* sacrifice for your sin, bearing wrath and entering hell for you, and when you are convinced that this Christ offers Himself in redeeming love to others who do not yet know Him, a passion will be lit in your heart to pursue a God-centered life.

---

* James Denney's address is in a compilation of his sermons under the title, *The Way Everlasting* (1911).

3
Ask for God's Help

There are no prizes for guessing that a book on 'How to navigate a God-centered life' will have something to say about prayer. But talking or writing about prayer is easier than praying, and that's where Jonah's confession is especially helpful.

This is the story of a mature believer who had stopped praying and, having stopped, did not know how to get started again. After his secret sin had been exposed, Jonah received revelation from God that the storm would cease if the crew threw him into the water. Jonah spoke to the crew about God. He preached and he prophesied but he could not bring himself to pray.

But a great transformation took place when Jonah was in the water. God broke through the barriers that had locked this man into despair. Hope was born and, out of that hope, Jonah began to pray.

I want you to see *how* this transformation happened. Discovering how a man who could not bring himself to pray finally got to the place where he called out to God will help you to foster prayer in your own life, and that will move you forward in navigating a God-centered life.

Sinking to the depths

In my distress I called to the LORD, and he answered me.
From the depths of the grave I called for help, and you listened to
my cry. (Jonah 2:2)

The trauma of being thrown into the raging sea remained so vivid in Jonah's mind that, long after the event, he could describe his experience in great detail.

When he first hit the water, Jonah worked hard to stay on the surface, but the currents kept pulling him under. Bobbing up and down, fighting for air and for his life, he managed to catch a breath, only to find another wave crashing over him, and taking him under again. With waves pounding him from above and currents pulling him from below, it wasn't long before Jonah went down.

Learning the story of Jonah as a child, I pictured God's extraordinary sea creature arriving to rescue the prophet as soon as he hit the water. But a closer look at the story has convinced me it wasn't like that.

God allowed Jonah to go to the bottom *before* He sent the fish. When, as Jonah says, "To the roots of the mountains I sank down" (v. 6), he clearly was no longer above the water. If Jonah could have stayed at the surface, he might have been able to hold on to some floating cargo and save himself. But God took Jonah down to the bottom, where he had no way out. His strength was gone; he was absolutely helpless. Then God sent the fish.

Have you ever found yourself in a situation where you felt completely overwhelmed? You tried to keep your head above water but the waves kept crashing over you, strong currents were pulling you under, and eventually your strength was gone.

Is this pounding really necessary? It was for Jonah. Resentment towards God had built up like a hard crust around his heart, and it took an extraordinary intervention to break the stronghold of this man's determined resistance to the Lord.

God had a great future in store for Jonah but none of it would have happened if it had not been for the raging storm, the tumbling dice and the pounding waves. Under God's almighty hand these were the means by which Jonah was brought to a place where, at last, he cried out to God for help.

Prayer is brought to birth through a continuing process in which three dynamics are always in play: awakening, believing and repenting. Take away any of these and prayer judders to a halt.

My aim in this chapter is to help you get the flywheel of prayer turning in your life. Living communion with God in which He is real, alive, fresh and present to your soul energizes a God-centered life. Jonah had lost this. He had become a discontented believer with his own agenda for life but, under the force of the pounding waves, his soul began to long for God.

Awakening: owning your true condition

You hurled me into the deep ... all your waves and breakers swept over me. (Jonah 2:3)

The first dynamic of prayer is an awakening in which you become aware of God laying hold of your life in a new way. When you are awakened you feel a sense of the greatness of life, the nearness of eternity, and the awesome holiness of God. At other times, the habits and compromises of your life seem like foibles to be taken in your stride but, when you are awakened, you feel a sense of your own sin and a desire to be different.

Awakening is a helpful word, because it describes what this experience is like. Jonah's sleeping on the boat was a symptom of the lethargy that had crept over his inner life. Once he had walked with God. As a prophet, he had enjoyed the privileged intimacy of receiving the words he spoke directly from the Lord. He had been God's man.

But something had gone wrong in Jonah's heart. The readiness he had known in his younger years to serve the Lord doing anything, anywhere, anytime, had given way to a more calculating form of service. Jonah had his terms and conditions. There were limits to what he was willing to do.

Spiritual decline often happens so slowly that you hardly notice. Worship becomes remote, prayer becomes repetitive, the Lord's Table becomes a habit, hearing the Word becomes routine, and your Christian life runs as if on automatic pilot. You are no longer engaged.

Gradually and increasingly a sense of unreality comes over your walk with the Lord. Cynicism, resentment and unbelief grow in your soul like weeds in a garden, but it all happens so slowly you hardly notice you are sleepwalking your way through the Christian life. That's where Jonah was until God sent the raging storm, the tumbling dice and the pounding waves.

It would not have been surprising if Jonah's resentment towards God had intensified when his plan for a new life in Tarshish was frustrated by the storm. Traumatic experiences often lead to long-term resentments: "Why did this happen to me? The dice are always loaded against me. Nobody cares about me. I hate my life." But that was not Jonah's reaction. Looking back on all that had happened, Jonah saw that God was working through these painful events in his life.

You *hurled me into the deep*. Your *waves swept over me*.
(Jonah 2:3)

Jonah could easily have said "The ship's crew threw me into the deep," but behind the human events, he saw the hand of God. It was God who had thrown him into the water. The waves that pushed him down were God's waves.

Some people see their lives as a series of events strung together by random chance and feel that their lives ride on luck. Others see their lives as a series of events controlled by other people and feel that they are victims. Others, again, feel in control of their lives and see themselves as heroes if things go well or as failures if they go badly. Jonah made none of these choices. Behind the crew and beyond the storm, Jonah knew that God was making an intervention in his life.

Recognizing God's hand in the painful events of his life was the first sign of a genuine change in Jonah. Previously, God had carried so little weight with him that Jonah could sleep comfortably while he was disobeying the Lord. Now, he knew that God was laying hold of his life. The haze and the stupor of his spiritual sleepwalk was gone. He felt God's presence and power. What had seemed vague, remote, dull and distant was now real, alive, fresh and present.

In this awakening, God gave Jonah a new sense of his own sin. Before the intervention, Jonah had been able to justify everything he had done. Resigning from his work was legitimate; heading for Tarshish was a reasonable course of action. Jonah had felt that he was within his rights and would have defended his decision. But when he was in the water, Jonah saw not only that God had sent the storm and the waves, but that it was right for God to do so.

When Jonah says "Your waves and breakers swept over me," he is not complaining as a man would if he felt God was treating him unfairly. He is *confessing* as a man does when he comes before God without evasion and without excuse. Jonah knew that he was in the water because of his own sin and rebellion against God. He had suppressed his guilt for a long time but, in the water, he saw his own sin clearly and knew that he was under the judgment of God.

One way to discern what's happening in your inner life right now is to ask yourself this question: Do you feel that God owes you something better than you have received? I find this a searching question. Living in a fallen world marked by sin, sickness and death, it is natural for us to look at our lives and wish that some things were different. Maybe you wish you had received different gifts, been given different opportunities, or enjoyed different experiences. But if you slide into thinking that God *owes* you something better than you received, you are making a big mistake.

Owning your sinfulness means getting beyond the idea that you deserve something better from God. God does not owe me a full and satisfying life. "The *wages* of sin is death" (Rom. 6:23). Wages are the payment due for work that has been done and, since I am a sinner by nature and practice, what I am owed is not an abundant life, but an eternal death. This is what I deserve from God. Anything else in this life or in the life to come is sheer mercy and grace.

Jonah saw this and owned it right there in the water. With the waves pouring over him, he was confessing, "God, these waves are *Your* waves. I am under *Your* judgment. And I *deserve* to be under Your judgment." Prayer begins with an awakening in which you own and confess your true position before God. God owes you nothing.

Believing: Battling for faith in Jesus Christ

I said, "I have been banished from your sight; yet I will look again toward your holy temple." (Jonah 2:4)

When God awakens you, the first danger you will face is the temptation to despair. When you feel the weight of your own sin and see its consequences in your life, darkness can set in, and hope can quickly die.

Maybe you have come to a place where you feel so bad about yourself and so desperate about the path of your life that prayer seems impossible. God seems far from you, and His hand seems to be against you. The pounding waves take their toll, and you feel yourself going under. That's where the second dynamic of prayer comes in: Prayer is given birth when an awakened person believes.

Before we look at Jonah's struggle to believe, we need to get a clear picture of where this battle took place: was it in the fish or was it in the water? Scripture records how Jonah prayed "from inside the fish" (Jonah 2:1). But the prayer that is recorded is in the past tense indicating that, while Jonah was thanking God for his deliverance inside the fish, he was also looking back on his experience in the water.

It was in the water that he said, "I have been banished from your sight," and it was in the water that he said, "yet I will look again toward your holy temple." This happened while the seaweed was wrapped around his head and as he was sinking to the roots of the mountains (vv. 4-5). It was out of the depths of this hell that he cried out to God for help (v. 2).

This might seem like a small point, but I think it is important. When Jonah was in the water he felt sure he would die. When he was in the fish he was sure he would live. The belly of the fish was not a place of trauma for Jonah; it was a place of deliverance. Despite the strangeness of the means, Jonah knew that God was saving him and once he was inside the fish, he worshiped God with thanksgiving, and declared that salvation comes from the Lord (v. 9).

His sudden awakening, desperate struggle for faith, and calling out to God all happened in the water. Later, when he was inside the fish, he looked back with wonder at how God had met him in these desperate moments and saved him from this watery hell.

Once awakened, Jonah had a *desire* to pray, but he still felt that God was so far from him that prayer would be impossible. Jonah's heart condemned him. He felt that he was beyond forgiveness and hope, so he said "I have been banished." A person banished from God's sight would no longer be in God's view or under His care, and Jonah came to a point where he believed that this was his position.

Even a mature believer can feel he has failed so badly that God would have no further interest in him.

But Jonah's despairing thought is not his only one. A battle rages in his soul while he struggles in the water. Faith rises within him, and he says, I'm going to cry out to God; I'm going to put my hope in Him. "Yet I will look again toward your holy temple." That is a glorious contradiction of what he had just said about being banished! It is a marvelous statement of faith, and it came out of the battle that was raging in Jonah's heart, right there in the water.

There will be times in your life when you want to pray but feel so far from God that prayer seems impossible. The flesh will tell you that God is against you, that you have gone too far and that He is no longer interested in you. But faith defies the flesh. It contradicts Satan's lies. It rises up against defeat, gloom and despair and finds hope in God.

Jonah didn't find it easy to trust God when he was struggling in the water. His faith came out of a great struggle between his own feelings of failure and the gracious promises of God. People sometimes speak about faith as if it were a small step, easily taken: "Just believe; put your trust in Jesus." But faith has enemies to overcome. It grapples like a wrestler with Satan's lies, so don't be surprised if the struggle to believe seems like the fight of your life.

Faith prevails over despair when you fix your eyes on the grace of God rather than your own failure. That's what Jonah was doing when he said, "I have been banished from your sight; *yet* I will look again toward your holy temple" (v. 4). When Jonah looked at himself, he despaired because he knew that he deserved to be banished. But then he dared to believe that there is hope in God and that he could find it by looking away from himself and his failures, and fixing his eyes on God and His grace.

'Looking' is a way of describing faith. The analogy goes back to an occasion when God's people were afflicted by venomous snakes during their years in the desert. With people all over the camp writhing in pain from the snake-bites, and losing strength by the minute, the Israelites asked Moses to pray. God told Moses to make a bronze snake and put it on a pole. Then He gave this promise: "Anyone who is bitten can *look* at it [the bronze snake] and live" (Num. 21:8).

Jesus used this story to help us understand what faith does. "Just as Moses lifted up the snake in the desert, so the Son of Man must be lifted up, that everyone who *believes* in him may have eternal life" (John 3:14-15). In using this picture, our Lord made it clear that faith involves believing that God delivers and trusting Him to do this for you *in the particular circumstances that you face*. Faith is exercised by looking away from yourself and your failure, and getting your eyes fixed on that grace and mercy which flow from Jesus Christ, crucified for you.

Don't miss the fact that Jonah was a mature believer, struggling to exercise faith. Faith is not a one-time decision. It is the bond of a living union with Jesus Christ in which you love, trust and follow Him, and that means that faith will always be in conflict with doubt and unbelief. The battle for faith will be the fight of your life. When you feel the weight of your own failure, you will find it especially difficult to believe that God has a future for you. Take Jonah as your example: "I said, I have been banished from your sight; *yet* I will look again toward your holy temple." Even though I am under God's judgment, I will dare to hope in Him. Make these words your own in your battle to believe.

Jonah's struggle for faith in the water is one of the great moments in the extraordinary drama of his life. His experience shows the shallowness of the popular idea that salvation is basically getting your act together through some moral effort, good works, family values, the Ten Commandments, and believing in Jesus along the way. God saves us because we cannot save ourselves. He sent the fish because Jonah had no other hope. What Jonah needed was not a belief but a deliverance; not a creed, but a Savior.

Did Jonah see the great sea creature coming? Was he conscious when he was swallowed, or had he already passed out? He doesn't tell us. But once inside the fish he breathes, like a man spluttering back to life from the brink of death. He was safe and he was overwhelmingly thankful.

Repenting: Releasing idols, laying hold of grace

Those who cling to worthless idols forfeit the grace that could be theirs. (Jonah 2:8)

Repentance is the third dynamic that gives birth to prayer and it is often misunderstood. Some think of it as a process in which you beat up on yourself. But Jesus said that there is *joy* in heaven over one sinner who repents. Why would there be joy in heaven over people beating up on themselves? What brings joy in heaven must bring joy on earth. So repentance is something to be sought and pursued.

Others see repentance as an event, carried out at the beginning of the Christian life and on subsequent occasions when you have obviously messed up, in which you admit that you are a sinner and tell God that you are sorry. But that misses the central point of the Christian life, which is that the Holy Spirit is continually making us more like Jesus.

Martin Luther said it well in the first of his famous ninety-five theses: "When our Lord and Master, Jesus Christ, said 'Repent,' He called us to a life of repentance."* A Christian never grows to the point where he or she is done with repenting. The Christian life is about us becoming like Christ and since that process will only be complete in heaven, repentance will be part of our experience throughout our life on earth.

Repentance and faith are two sides of the same coin. Neither can exist without the other. We repent believingly and believe penitently. Repentance is possible only when faith is present and where there is faith, repentance will also be found. Faith gives birth to repentance, and repentance is the evidence of faith.

Repentance means change: Change in what you think, change in what you desire, change in what you do and say. It is the evidence of authentic faith.

Jonah repented *inside* the fish. In the water, he felt banished from the sight of God, and struggled against despair. But Jonah put his hope in God, and God sent the fish to save him.

The fish gives us a wonderful picture of what it means to be 'in Christ.' Imaginative story tellers may go to town on how terrible it must have been for Jonah to endure three days in the belly of this great sea creature, but Jonah never complained about being inside the fish. When he was in the

---

* See http://www.spurgeon.org/~phil/history/95theses.htm

water he felt sure he would die, but once he was inside the fish, he knew he would live. Inside the fish, Jonah knew that he was safe. God had delivered him and it was *here* that he got down to the serious business of repenting.

Inside the fish, Jonah made choices and commitments that reflected the change God was bringing in his heart. The man who had set out for Tarshish, now saw that his dream of a self-determined life was an idol that had caused him to miss what God was ready to give. Like a child whose hand is stuck in the jar because he is grasping a cookie that he refuses to let go, Jonah found that the idol he had cherished had trapped him and only by letting it go would he be free to receive what God had in store. Jonah released the idol of his self-governed life, and made a new pledge of obedience to God, "What I have vowed I will make good" (v. 9).

For many years, I thought of repentance as a gateway to grace. Like many others, I had the idea that repentance comes before faith and that you have to abandon your sins in order to believe. But think this through: Faith is the bond of a living union with Jesus Christ. If God required repentance *before* you came to faith you would have to do it in your own power. How would that be possible? Where would you find the inclination and the ability to change?

It is a great mistake to make repentance a work that we need to do in order to receive the grace of God. That can only lead to despair. God would be asking you to do something that is beyond your ability. It would be like saying to a drowning man: "If you swim to the shore, I will send you a lifeboat." The idea is ridiculous. The drowning man needs a lifeboat precisely because he cannot swim to the shore.

The good news is that God does not ask us to change so that we can come to Christ. He invites us to come to Christ so that we can change. Repentance is a gift of God (Acts 11:18). It flows from faith, and faith flows from a spiritual awakening to your own need and to God's glory.

The repentance that Jonah could not find in the boat was God's gift to him in the fish. This is an important insight for grasping *how* God brings change in the life of a Christian believer. Grace makes repentance possible.

The man who had refused God's call, had been unable to pray on the ship, and who had felt banished from God in the water found repentance in the fish, and began to worship. "I, with a song of thanksgiving, will sacrifice to you" (v. 9). Inside the fish was surely a strange venue for worship, but God's grace had brought such a transformation in Jonah's life that the highest worship ascended from the darkest place.

Putting these pieces together, you can see that a profound change was taking place in Jonah's life. He saw that his dream had become an idol and that it had to be smashed so that his hands would be free to receive what God had in store for him. The stubborn heart that had kept him running from God was changing. A new love, freedom and joy in God were rising in his soul. He had a new desire to honor, serve and obey the Lord, and all of this flowed from God's grace that He was receiving through faith while he was in the belly of the fish. By grace, through faith, in Christ—that's how real and lasting change happens, and that's where prayer begins.

The chief exercise of faith

Over the years I've found much of what I've read about prayer to be unhelpful. Here's why: Prayer is usually considered under the heading of 'spiritual disciplines' which makes it the spiritual equivalent of running on a treadmill or flossing your teeth, neither of which are attractive to me. Viewing prayer purely as a discipline drags the whole business back into the world of law, and law can never impart life.

I awakened to this when I discovered a description of prayer that warmed my heart with a fresh desire to pray. Calvin describes prayer as "the chief exercise of faith by which we daily receive God's benefits." Then he offers this compelling picture: "We dig up by prayer the treasures that were pointed out by the Lord's gospel, and which our faith has gazed upon." * Imagine walking over a field where vast treasure lies buried. To make these riches your own, you need two things: a map and a spade. Scripture is your map, and prayer is your spade.

I find this picture helpful because it delivers prayer from the austere world of law and discipline and brings it into the realm of the gospel and promise, where it belongs. Prayer is more than a duty to be fulfilled; it is a gift to be enjoyed. There is a world of a difference between 'having your quiet time' as a spiritual discipline and drawing near to God to possess what He promises to you in Christ.

Since prayer is "the chief exercise of faith by which we daily receive God's benefits," it follows that the *primary* gifts you will receive go far beyond 'answers' to items or needs on your prayer list. Prayer is the means by which you lay hold of all that God has promised in your own life and in the lives of others for whom you pray.

---

* *Institutes*, Book 3, Chapter 20.

I've found this insight especially helpful. If you are like me, you will often find it difficult to know what to ask for in prayer. God knows what He is doing in any given situation. I don't. What I, and others for whom I pray, need most is not a particular outcome to the problem being faced, but the ability to stand, to endure and to bear fruit in any circumstance of life. Prayer does not give you the power to dictate the outcome of events. It is the means by which you appropriate God's grace for the circumstances of life that you face.

Many Christians struggle with a sense of unreality in their spiritual lives. Football, friendships, and finances are tangible and immediately enjoyable, but the blessings of the gospel sometimes seem more distant, vague, and detached from the realities of daily life. That's not surprising. The blessings of the gospel *are* hidden, and prayer is the means by which we dig them up! Through prayer a sense of God's love, patience, kindness, power, and peace are made real, alive, fresh and present in your soul. Through prayer you lay hold of all that is yours in Christ: forgiveness, hope, strength, freedom, and joy, so that you may savor and rejoice in all that is yours in Jesus Christ. If you don't use the spade, the treasure will remain buried.

Prayer is the chief exercise of faith. So if you are not praying, what does it mean to say that you are believing? It is possible to walk over the gospel field with a spade in your hand and yet never dig up the treasure to make it your own. Thinking about that folly makes me want to open my Bible and pray.

4
Believe God's Word

Some years ago, I was asked by a couple in England to perform their wedding service. It was to be held in a beautiful ancient church—a picture perfect location for their happy day. The bride and groom both loved the Lord and had been praying for their respective families, most of whom were unbelievers. "We want you to do the wedding," they said, "and we want you to preach the gospel. It will be a great opportunity." So we planned the service, including time for a fifteen-minute sermon.

My wife came with me along with our son Andrew, who was just a baby at the time. He became unsettled during the sermon and Karen took him out to the church entrance, where the photographer was pacing up and down like a caged lion. He hadn't planned on waiting through a sermon and he was anxious for the service to end so that he could take his pictures and get on to his next appointment.

"Who is that man who is going on, and on, and on?" he asked in exasperation. To which Karen replied, "Oh, that's my husband!"

The photographer turned a bright shade of red and was relieved to discover that my wife has a great sense of humor. "Wait till I tell *my* wife about this!" he said.

I laughed when Karen told me, but the photographer's words have stayed in my mind. For many people, a sermon is simply some person going on, and on, and on. Every Sunday, thousands of Christians gather for worship. The people sing, an offering is usually taken, and then someone stands up to speak. What is this and why do we do it? When the preacher speaks what should he be saying? And what good can it do?

This chapter is about the Word of God, and its place in your pursuit of a God-centered life. God will nourish your spiritual life through your *reading* of His Word in private and your *hearing* of His Word in public.

At the heart of Jonah's story is the remarkable account of how a pagan city was transformed by the preaching of God's Word. Jonah's adventure began when "The word of the LORD" came to him (Jonah 1:1). Then, after the trauma of his dramatic rescue, we are told that "the word of the LORD came to Jonah a second time" (Jonah 3:1).

What is the 'word' of the Lord? How did it come to Jonah and the other prophets? And how does God speak today? These are the questions before us in this chapter.

Why the Bible is different from any other book
The place to begin is with the claim that Scripture makes for itself: "All Scripture is God-breathed" (2 Tim. 3:16).

The words you read in the Bible did not have their origin with Moses, David, Isaiah, or Jonah. God breathed out His Word and He spoke it through the apostles and prophets. That makes the Bible different from any other book.

Visit any bookstore or library and you will find a vast selection of writings covering religion, spirituality, and philosophy, in which men and women speak about God. Many people have bought into the idea that, since these writings reflect insights from different cultures, it would be arrogant for anyone to claim that their religious writings are better than the thoughts or insights of others. Religion, they claim, is a private matter and each of us has to find his or her own way.

One analogy for this view is that we are all like ants on the back of an elephant. Each of the ants has a perception of the elephant, but at the end of the day, the elephant is simply too large for any of the ants to know. The point of the analogy is that, like the ants, we are scratching around with our tiny insights into God, who is ultimately unknowable.

But what if the elephant could speak in a language that ants could understand? What if the elephant said, "Let me tell you about my trunk and tusks that you have never seen." What if it were to say, "Let me tell you where I am going and what I will do." The words of the elephant would be *in a different category* from all the insights, speculations and experiences of the ants.

This is precisely what the Scriptures claim: God Himself has spoken. The words of Scripture are not our words about God, but God's words to us in which He makes Himself known. The words of Scripture are therefore different from any other words. The Bible is different from any other book, and God's revelation to us is different from all human thought about Him.

How the prophets received the Word of God

The apostle Peter gives us a glimpse into what it was like for the prophets to receive the words that God breathed out. He begins by clearing away the most common misunderstanding of the Bible—that its words had their origin in the minds and hearts of men.

> *No prophecy of Scripture came about by the prophet's own interpretation. For prophecy never had its origin in the will of man* (2 Peter 1:20).

By referring to "prophecy of Scripture," Peter makes it clear that he is referring to the Old Testament, and he distinguishes the "prophecy of Scripture" from all other prophecy.

It's easy to claim that you have a message from God, though if you had lived in ancient Israel you would have thought twice before making that claim. The penalty for being a false prophet (that is claiming that a message came from God when it really was only your own thought) was stoning.

There weren't many things you could get stoned for in Israel but this was one of them, and the reason for the severity of this law was that it is no small thing to claim the authority of God for your own ideas. That's worth remembering if you are in the habit of talking easily about how the Lord told you this, that and the other. If you had done that in ancient Israel you might have found yourself up for a hearing before the elders; and if they concluded that you were claiming God's authority for your own ideas, you wouldn't be making any more statements about what the Lord had told you!

In ancient Israel, God's people knew that there was a world of difference between the thoughts of men and the Word of God. We need to understand that distinction today.

Every year thousands of books (including this one) are published. They were written because the author felt that he or she had something to say, and someone agreed to publish their work. The book came from a man or woman's initiative and creativity. The words are those of the author, and they reflect his or her insights.

The world is full of books about God, and history is littered with various interpretations of life. There's the communist view, the fascist view, the Islamic view, the new age view, the environmental view, the liberal view, the conservative view, and so on. So it's natural for people to look at the Bible and assume that this is another view to be added to the list.

But Peter says, "Scripture isn't like that!" Don't put the Old Testament prophets in the long list of interpretations of God, life, meaning and existence that people are pushing in the world today. The prophets don't belong in that line up. They're different! *No prophecy of Scripture came about by the prophet's own interpretation, for prophecy never had its origin in the will of man!*

Carried along by the wind of the Holy Spirit
So how did the prophets receive the words that God had spoken?

Prophecy never had its origin in the will of man, but men spoke from God as they were carried along by the Holy Spirit (2 Peter 1:21).

The best way to grasp what Peter is saying here is through a story, recorded in the book of Acts about a time when the apostle Paul was taken by ship, as a prisoner, to Rome.

During the journey, the ship ran into a wind of hurricane force called the 'northeaster.' Luke, who was travelling with Paul, records, "The ship was caught by the storm and could not head into the wind; so we gave way to it and were driven along" (Acts 27:15).

The word used by Luke for the ship being 'driven along' by the wind is the same word that Peter used for the prophets being 'carried along' by the Spirit. The direction of the boat was controlled by the wind. The words of the prophets were controlled by the Spirit.

The prophets did not control the message; the message controlled them. It came to them from God like a mighty wind, and they were carried along in it so that what they wrote was exactly what God wanted them to say. God breathed His Word through David's songs, through Job's sorrow, and through commandments given to Moses, in such a way that these men spoke from God.

When you read the Scripture, you are reading the Word of God. The words you read are God's words to you. When you hear these words, you are hearing the voice of God. This is how He speaks to you.

Placing yourself under the Word of God

Since God's Word is different from any other word, it makes sense to approach the Scriptures in a way that is different from any other book. When I read a book, I try to learn from the author, but I always reserve the right to disagree. Books do not have authority over me. The book is in my hands and I am free to form an opinion of it, and sometimes against it.

But the Bible is different because it is the Word of God, by which He speaks to me. Disagreeing with the Bible would be disagreeing with God. So when I read the Bible I want to place myself 'under' it. I want to receive the Scripture in such a way that over time, my thinking, feeling, choosing, believing and behaving will be molded by the Word God is speaking into my life. I don't want to critique the Scriptures; I want them to critique me and change me.

The story of Jonah's ministry in Nineveh gives a marvelous sample of how God changes people through His Word. "The word of the LORD came to Jonah" (Jonah 3:1). He received the Word, and was driven along by it, just as Peter described. He went to the city and proclaimed the Word God had given; and when the people heard it, they believed God, called on Him and gave up their evil and violent ways. The Word brought *faith*, it ignited *prayer*, and it produced *repentance* in people who had no prior interest in God. By any standards, that is a remarkable transformation and it all happened through the Word of God.

How God changes people through His Word

> On the first day, Jonah started into the city. He proclaimed: "Forty more days and Nineveh will be overturned." (Jonah 3:4).

People in the great cities of the world live relentless lives, consumed with our immediate concerns: running a business, raising a family, and enjoying some sport. Jonah walked into the intense activity of a large city and said, "Forty more days and Nineveh will be overturned."

Authentic gospel preaching always engages people with eternal issues. It lifts our horizons from the immediate interests of our lives to the imminent and overwhelming reality of eternal life or everlasting destruction.

The church I serve recently acquired a museum that we adapted for use as a ministry campus. Too many churches have become museums and so it's about time a museum became a church! It took about a year to complete the renovations. Finally the day came for our public launch.

I try to set a schedule well in advance for the passages of Scripture that will be preached in our services. When our team told me the date they had targeted for the public launch of the new campus, I checked the schedule and found that the Scripture set for that day included the following verses:

> *God is just ... He will punish those who do not know God and do not obey the gospel of our Lord Jesus. ... They will be punished with everlasting destruction and shut out from the presence of the Lord ...* (2 Thess. 1:6, 8-9)

That's a long way from "Four ways to have a happy and fulfilling life," and it's hardly what you would choose to make a good impression on first time visitors to a newly opened church! The pressure to drop these difficult words and choose something more appealing was real. But it would have been a great mistake.

I swallowed hard and told the crowd of several hundred who came that, long before we knew the date of the opening, these verses had been set for the day. I told them honestly that it is often tempting for a pastor to fit the message to what people want to hear, but that helps none of us. We need to hear what God has to say, especially when it makes us feel uncomfortable. The day was marked by God's blessing, with great joy at the amazing grace of God who delivers us from everlasting destruction through His Son, and with renewed resolve that we should bring this good news to others.

The awful reality of the judgment of God is a banner headline without which the story of God's redeeming love would often go unread. John the Baptist began his ministry with a simple message: "Prepare the way for the Lord" (Mark 1:3). "You are going to meet with God," he was saying. God is coming, and you will have to give an account to Him. People understood this message and they went out to him, confessing their sins, and being baptized.

Our Lord began His public ministry on the same note: "The kingdom of God is near. Repent and believe the good news" (Mark 1:15). When Paul laid out his most organized presentation of the gospel, he also began with the awful reality of the judgment of God: "The wrath of God is being revealed from heaven against all the godlessness and wickedness of men" (Rom. 1:18).

Jonah began there too: "Forty more days and Nineveh will be overturned" (v. 4). "Whatever you are doing now," he was saying, "you need to realize you will soon face the judgment of God. You can defy God for a time, but in the end you have to face Him and that day is nearer than you think. Forty more days and Nineveh will be overturned."

I don't suppose this was the only thing that Jonah said, but that was the core of his message, and everyone knew it.

The people of Nineveh knew that there was a prophet in town and his message was, "Forty more days and Nineveh will be overturned." God took that one sentence and burned it into the minds and hearts of the people.

Flawed messengers who have experienced grace

It's clear to me that Jonah told the people of Nineveh the extraordinary story of God's grace in his own life, and that God used what had happened to him for their eternal good. I believe this for two reasons. The first is that the king said: "Who knows? God may yet relent and with compassion turn from his fierce anger so that we will not perish" (v. 9).

Where did the king get that idea? If all Jonah had said was, "Forty more days and Nineveh will be destroyed," why would the king have any reason to hope in the mercy and compassion of God? But if the king knew Jonah's story, he would have reason to say, "If God saved Jonah, perhaps He will have compassion on us."

The second reason I believe Jonah told them his story is this: when our Lord applied the story of Jonah, He said, "As Jonah was a sign to the Ninevites, so also will the Son of Man be to this generation" (Luke 11:30). Jonah, the man himself, was a sign to the Ninevites. But in what sense was he a sign? Some people say it is simply the sign of a man preaching, but Jesus says something more:

> *A wicked and adulterous generation asks for a miraculous sign! But none will be given it except the sign of the prophet Jonah. For as Jonah was three days and three nights in the belly of a huge fish, so the Son of Man will be three days and three nights in the heart of the earth.* (Matt. 12:39-40)

Jonah was a sign to the Ninevites, and the sign was that he was three days and three nights in the belly of a fish. That must mean that he told them his story.

When Jonah proclaimed the Word of God, he must have preached with a special passion born from his own experience. God's judgment was coming, and the man who announced it had experienced that judgment in his own life, and yet had found mercy.

"Forty more days and Nineveh will be destroyed – I know what I am talking about. Let me tell you what happened to me! I have worshiped the God I am telling you about all my life. But when He called me to come here, I refused. I thought I could disobey Him and get away with it.

"I got on a boat and headed for Tarshish, but God sent a storm. God's judgment had come on me. I felt sure I was finished, and I told the crew to throw me overboard. When I hit the water I was sure it would only be moments before I drowned, but God had compassion on me. The God whose judgment I deserved saved me!

"Now He has sent me here to tell you that your wickedness has come up before Him, just as mine did. Forty more days and Nineveh will be destroyed."

And the king says, "If the Lord had mercy on Jonah, maybe He will have mercy on us."

Here's what you can take from this: God uses flawed messengers who have experienced His grace. He will use what He has been doing in your life as a means of reaching others. God never wastes a thing. He can use your failures, your traumas, your shame, and the most desperate moments of your life to advance the gospel. Sinclair Ferguson says it beautifully: "The jewels of spiritual service are always quarried in the depths of spiritual experience."*

Hearing and believing

The Ninevites believed God. They declared a fast, and all of them, from the greatest to the least, put on sackcloth. (Jonah 3:5)

When Jonah spoke God's Word, the Ninevites knew that God was speaking. They heard Jonah; they believed God. The Holy Spirit gave weight to the Word and, through its living power, He changed the hearts of people who had no previous interest in the things of God. The simplicity of what Jonah did in speaking God's Word is striking; the power of what God did through His Word is astounding.

The pressure is always on the church to make the message about issues that the unbeliever can connect with. The argument is simple: People aren't interested in the Bible; they aren't thinking about eternity. We must start where people are and connect with unbelieving people by giving them something they can relate to, something that grabs their interest and relates to their concerns – work, family, friendship and purpose.

This argument has some force. It is obviously true that unbelievers have little interest in hearing the gospel. They don't want it and they can't understand it. The Scripture tells us that unbelievers "cannot see the light of the gospel of the glory of Christ" (2 Cor. 4:4). So what's the point of speaking to unbelievers about a Christ whose glory they cannot see?

---

* Sinclair B. Ferguson, *Man Overboard!* (Banner of Truth, 2008), p. 84.

When Christ is lifted up, He draws people to Himself. God uses the proclamation of Jesus as Lord to make His light "shine in our hearts to give us the light of the knowledge of the glory of God in the face of Christ" (2 Cor. 4:6).

God gives light to darkened human hearts *through the gospel*. Faith comes through hearing the Word, and even the capacity to hear the Word is given as it is proclaimed (Rom. 10:17). Here lies the great paradox of ministry: If we preach a message that the unbeliever can understand, God's light will not shine and the unbeliever will remain in darkness. But when we proclaim the glory of Christ that the unbeliever cannot see, God will shine His light into the dark recesses of some unbelieving hearts, creating faith and understanding through the Word that honors His Son.

To put it simply: If we preach what the unbeliever *can* see, he or she *won't* see. We must preach what the unbeliever *can't* see, so that he or she *will* see.

Not everyone who hears the gospel will be saved. Some remain in darkness. But God shines His light into human hearts *through the gospel*. It is in this way that people come to see the light of the knowledge of the glory of God in the face of Jesus Christ.

What God did in Nineveh was by any standards extraordinary, and so we need to apply what we learn from this story carefully. It would be a great mistake, for example, to suggest that ministry can only be done by a man with a Bible proclaiming a message that can be reduced to a single sentence. But by isolating the clear proclamation of His Word, God is surely telling us that *this is the means by which*

He does His saving work. The Spirit transforms human lives through the Word.

The work of evangelism may be approached in many creative ways, but whatever is done to engage people's interest and attention, it is *the Word itself* that brings life, faith, prayer and repentance. God's Word is the living seed that brings new birth. It is the milk that nurtures the new life of a young Christian and the meat that builds the muscle of a mature believer.

In every area of ministry we must ask: How is God's Word present? What truth of Scripture is being presented? Is it clear? Have people heard who God is, what sin is, and who Christ is? Has there been a clear statement of how He offers Himself and all that He has accomplished in his death and resurrection to sinners? Is it clear that a person must embrace Christ in faith and repentance? And is it plain that in doing this, a person gives unconditional command of his or her life to Christ and can never be the same again?

The Bible as a ministry strategy

Some years ago, I received a call asking that the elders of our church should go and pray with a couple who were in deep crisis. When we arrived in the home it was immediately evident that the problems were severe. The home was chaotic, the marriage was at breaking point, the wife was depressed, the husband had withdrawn and the kids were out of control.

God's work of grace in this couple has been marvelous to see. In these last years, their marriage has been blessed, their business has prospered, and order has been restored in their home. Karen and I recently enjoyed an evening with them. Over dinner, I recalled the scene when the elders had visited, and we all rejoiced in the dramatic change that had taken place since that time. "Tell me how this happened," I asked.

The wife recalled how her mentor from the church had come to her home after the elders had prayed. "I dumped everything on her," she said, "everything that was wrong with my life—I just let her have it."

The mentor had listened for a long time, and then said, gently, but firmly, "Here's what you need to do: Get up in the morning, read your Bible and pray, and I will help you to apply what you learn. If you are willing to do that I will walk with you." The two women walked together, reading, believing and applying the Word of God. The men did the same. Over time, the Word did its work and the family was transformed.

If you find this simplistic, I plead with you to ask yourself why. Could it be that you have lost confidence in the power of the Scriptures?

Christians believe that the Bible is God's Word, but many are not yet convinced that the Bible does God's work. So having affirmed their belief in Scripture, they plunge into pragmatic discussions about ministry models that will 'work.' What will bring real life change?

King David had a higher view of Scripture.

The law of the LORD is perfect,
    reviving the soul.
The statutes of the LORD are trustworthy,
    making wise the simple.

The precepts of the LORD are right,
  giving joy to the heart.
The commands of the LORD are radiant,
  giving light to the eyes.

(Ps. 19:7-8)

David was convinced, not only that God's Word is perfect, trustworthy, right and radiant, but that God *uses* this Word to revive the soul, make the simple wise, give joy to the heart and light to the eyes. If you share David's conviction, you will see that the Bible is more than an authoritative book. It is a ministry strategy. God's Word does God's work. When you see this and believe it, you will put the Scripture at the center of your life and your ministry.

Next time you have the opportunity to help a friend who is in great spiritual need, consider taking a book of the Bible and reading it together, section by section, believing, applying and repenting as you go. Plant the seed of the Word, water it with your prayers and see what happens. Try it. I dare you.

In serving as a pastor for over thirty years, I have seen some remarkable transformations and I've seen some big disappointments. I have two observations. First, where there has been lasting life change, the common factor, in every case, is that the Word of God has had a significant entrance into the person's life. Second, where godly change has failed to get started, or has slowly unraveled, the common factor, in every case, is that change has been attempted without significant engagement in the Scriptures.

If you are inclined to think of the Bible primarily as information, please think again. It is food. It is medicine. It has life-giving power. It is the sword that the Spirit uses in the great battles against sin in your life. It is the means by which God communicates Himself to your soul.

So do all you can to make sure that God's Word has a significant entrance into your life. Make a plan for regular reading of the Scriptures. Read books by authors who place the Bible in authority over themselves and avoid books by authors who place themselves in authority over the Bible.

Do everything in your power to find a church where the Bible is taught, believed and applied. Many Christians make their choice of a church in large measure through the music, or the style. That's rather like choosing a restaurant on the basis of the décor or the seating. What matters in choosing a restaurant is the quality of the food. Is it nourishing? Is it well prepared? Will it make you strong, or could it make you sick? God's Word nourishes the soul, so find a church where you will be fed on a healthy diet of Christ-exalting, biblical truth. Commit yourself to that church, find a way to get involved in ministry there and you will be greatly helped in pursuing a God-centered life.

5
Affirm God's Grace

There is a particular darkness that sometimes comes to those who work hardest in the Lord's service. Resentment towards God is the special temptation of mature believers who serve Him well. Most pastors and missionaries know about this: The more you do for God, the easier it is to feel that God owes you. So if you stretch yourself out in serving God, don't be surprised when this strange darkness sneaks up on you. You *will* encounter this trial, and you need to know how to deal with it.

Jonah experienced this strange darkness of soul. He was a mature believer, a cross-cultural missionary and a preacher of God's Word. You might expect that a man who has experienced miracles in his personal life and revival through his ministry would be full of joy and thanksgiving. Not Jonah. After all the triumphs of God's grace in his experience, Jonah was angry, frustrated and out of sorts with God.

There's a profound mystery here: How is it possible to serve God and end up resenting Him? By what strange contradiction do I experience God's grace in my life and yet *still* struggle with the God I love? This was Jonah's experience and he is not alone.

Asaph was King David's music director. He walked with God and led God's people in worship but, like Jonah, he went through a dark experience in which, he says,

> *My feet had almost slipped;*
> *I had nearly lost my foothold.*
> (Ps. 73:2)

Asaph's crisis of confidence followed a simple pattern. He saw that God allows the wicked to prosper, and he couldn't figure out why. The more he thought about it, the more it perplexed him. God seemed to be kinder to His enemies than to His friends, and this raised a profound question for Asaph: What is the point of struggling to live a holy life when God takes no action against the wicked? If God allows evil men to prosper, why should I keep my heart pure?

The elder brother in our Lord's parable of the Prodigal Son had a similar problem. This man worked hard for his father, while his no-good brother left home and wasted the family inheritance on riotous living. Then, when the self-indulgent wretch came home, the Father forgave him and threw a party! Where's the justice in that?

Jonah, Asaph and the elder brother were all in the same place: They were angry with God about grace.

Angry with God about grace

Jonah was greatly displeased and became angry. (Jonah 4:1)

God's people have celebrated His grace from earliest times. This was the heart of what God revealed to Moses when he went up the mountain to receive the commandments for the second time. God passed in front of Moses, speaking glorious words of self-description:

The LORD, The LORD, the compassionate and gracious God, slow to anger, abounding in love and faithfulness, maintaining love to thousands, and forgiving wickedness, rebelliousness and sin. (Exod. 34:6-7).

God proclaimed His grace to Moses immediately after the rebellion in which God's people had worshiped a golden calf. The people knew that they were sinners in need of God's mercy, and they received His grace with gladness. They cherished the words God had spoken to Moses and, through the centuries that followed, used them in worship as an ascription of praise. Everyone in Israel knew that God is gracious and compassionate, slow to anger and abounding in love.

But Jonah had a problem. He felt that God was *too* slow to anger, *too* passive in dealing with evil, so he took up the great affirmation of grace given to Moses, and turned it back to God as a complaint:

O LORD, is this not what I said when I was still at home? That is why I was so quick to flee to Tarshish. I knew that you are a gracious and compassionate God, slow to anger and abounding in love, a God who relents from sending calamity (Jonah 4:2).

Nineveh had a long history of wickedness, and Jonah felt sure that the Ninevites would return to type, even if they repented for a time. He was right. The people who repented were soon replaced by a generation who went back to the old ways of violence and torture. Just forty years after Jonah's ministry in Nineveh, the ten tribes in the northern kingdom of Israel were crushed and scattered by brutal Assyrian aggression.[*]

The book of Nahum describes the atrocities of that time:

> *Many casualties,*
> *piles of dead,*
> *bodies without number*
> *people stumbling over the corpses …*
>
> (Nahum 3:3)

All of this suffering could have been avoided, if only God had destroyed Nineveh in the time of Jonah. The prophet saw this coming and God's mercy made him mad!

It isn't hard to relate to Jonah's problem. If God had wiped out Hitler, or Stalin or Osama Bin Laden when they were young, the world would have been spared unspeakable evil and suffering. But God let them live! Why? Because He is "gracious and compassionate … slow to anger and abounding in love." That was Jonah's complaint.

If you have experienced a great evil in your life, it may be your complaint too. God could have intervened to stop that evil from happening, but He didn't. He allowed it, and you suffered.

Grace means that God may bless people who have wronged you, people from whose sins you have suffered. When that happens, you may find yourself asking, "Why doesn't God give them what they deserve?" Sometimes God seems to bless the wrong people. His grace seems misdirected.

---

[*] Walter Kaiser dates Jonah's ministry c. 780–765 B.C. (*A History of Israel* [Broadman & Holman Publishers, 1998], p. 354). The scattering of the ten northern tribes was in 722 B.C.

God needs no permission

To many Christians, grace simply means that God is generous and kind to everyone, that He sent His Son to die for our sins, and that through Him, God has opened a way of salvation for everyone who wants to receive it. If this was the full extent of God's grace, no-one would be angry. But there's more, much more.

Grace means that God has free will. He steps into the lives of particular individuals with the purpose and effect of saving them. God needs no permission to do this, nor is He under any obligation to do so. God has total freedom and He uses it: "Our God is in heaven; he does whatever pleases him" (Ps. 115:3).

I want to help you grapple with this description of grace, to work through the problems and objections that may come to your mind and to share with you the blessings I've found in affirming God's grace. So let's ponder this description of grace together:

God steps into the lives of particular individuals with the purpose and effect of saving them. Without this intervention in your life and mine, neither of us would have any hope of being saved. By nature, no one seeks God. Not you, and not me. No one.

The Bible is very clear about this:

There is no one who understands, no one who seeks God.
(Rom. 3:11)

The idea that we have the inclination and capacity in ourselves to go seeking after God is completely foreign to the Bible. *All have turned away* (Rom. 3:12). The human endeavor described as 'seeking God' is often a smokescreen for avoiding Him, and the most comprehensive demon-stration of this tragic reality can be seen in the world's religions, where what we call seeking God turns out to be avoiding Him on a man-made religious path.

The root of our reluctance to seek after God lies in the debilitating effect of sin on the human soul. By nature, I do not see the glory of Christ (2 Cor. 4:4). By nature my heart is hard towards God (Ezek. 36:26). By nature, I love darkness rather than light (John 3:19). By nature I want the praise of men more than the affirmation of God (John 5:44). By nature I am a prisoner of sin (Rom. 7:23). The list goes on and on.

When you grasp this biblical teaching about the effects of sin on the human soul, it will become obvious to you that grace must involve more than God providing a way of salvation. It has to be about God stepping into the lives of particular individuals to save them. Grace is more than God opening the door to salvation; it's God bringing people in.

God came looking for Abraham, when he was worship-ing idols and knew nothing about God (Josh. 24:2-3). He set His love on Israel, for no other reason than that He chose to love them (Deut. 7:7-8). If you are in Christ today, the ultimate explanation is that He set His love on you. God came after you and found you. You came to repentance and faith because God came looking for you *before* you were looking for Him. That's grace, and it is by grace that you have been saved (Eph. 2:8).

To me, the most obvious demonstration of God's free-dom to step uninvited into human lives is the story of Saul of Tarsus. This man was the terror of the early church. Having supervised the death of Stephen, the first Christian martyr, Saul was on his way to Damascus where he planned to initiate a campaign of violence against a small community of believers.

Saul set out on his journey "breathing out murderous threats against the Lord's disciples" (Acts 9:1). That's pretty intense hostility. He was in the same mindset as a terrorist who might seek the slaughter of Christians worshiping in a small church today. One thing is certain; Saul was not seeking faith in Jesus Christ. The idea would have been repugnant to him.

Christ stopped this man in his tracks with a blinding light and an audible voice on the road to Damascus. "Saul, Saul, why do you persecute me?" (Acts 9:4). Saul was not looking for Jesus, but Jesus came looking for him and Saul the persecutor became Paul the apostle. It was an amazing transformation.

The point here is that Christ did not need permission to intervene in Saul's life. That permission would never have been given! Christ swooped into this man's life *uninvited*. That's grace, and without it nobody would be saved. Our seeking after God is always the effect of His seeking after us.

God, that's not fair!
So far, this all sounds like good news, and you may be wondering why grace would make anyone angry. So let's probe a little further: Grace means that God steps into the lives of particular individuals with the purpose and effect of saving them. He needs no permission to do this, *nor is He under any obligation to do so*.

Most people would not object to the idea of God stepping into people's lives in order to save them. The problem comes with the fact that while God does this in the lives of some, He does not do it in the lives of all.

Grace says, "Jacob I loved ... Esau I hated" (Rom. 9:13). These six words have caused massive problems for many people, but their meaning is really quite clear. God is absolutely free to go after Jacob and save him and He has no obligation to do the same for Esau.

How do you feel about that? Is there an instinct in you that wants to say to God, "It's fine for You to love Jacob, but You have to do the same for Esau as well"?

Loving Jacob and not doing the same for Esau seems unfair, and Paul faces this problem head on:

What then shall we say? Is God unjust? Not at all!
For [God] says to Moses, "I will have mercy on whom I have
mercy, and I will have compassion on whom I have compassion."
(Rom. 9:14-15)

Do you see what God is saying? He reserves the right to decide where, when and on whom He will have mercy. This is His business, not ours. There is no right to mercy. The rapist cannot command mercy from his victim, and sinners have no right to mercy from the God we have offended. Mercy is God's gift. It is not our right.

An expression of our sinful pride is that we make so much of our own freedom and so little of God's. We feel that we must be free to choose or reject Him, but we do not feel that He should be free to choose or reject us. If God were under an obligation to save everyone He would no longer be God, because a law higher than Himself would bind him, and mercy would no longer be mercy because, being required, it could no longer be freely given.

The biblical defense of the justice of God is not that God gives everyone an equal opportunity to be saved. It is:

1. that God is under no obligation to save anyone;

2. that God is free to do whatever pleases Him;

3. that when God saves, He always does so on the basis of absolute justice, drawing sinners through faith, into union with Christ, whose blood was shed as a propitiation for their sins (Rom. 3:23-25).

The obvious conclusion to all this is that salvation "does not, therefore, depend on man's desire or effort, but on God's mercy" (Rom. 9:16). You are saved, not because you had a desire to be saved, or because you made an effort to be saved. Your salvation flows from God mercifully intervening in your life and moving you to faith and repentance.

Children of a lesser God

It's not surprising that some Christians feel more comfortable with a lesser form of grace, in which God opens the door of salvation without doing anything to bring particular individuals in.

But this account of grace makes God less and us more. If your salvation rested ultimately on your response to an offer from God, in which He treats all people exactly the same, you would have saved yourself by virtue of being smart enough to recognize a good deal, and wise enough to take advantage of it. You would be saved by making a better choice than the person who was lost. And, since you stood on a level playing field, that has to make you the better person. Notice how grace just disappeared.

But it's worse than that. If God opened the door of salvation and then stood back, leaving the rest up to us, nobody would be saved. Grace that opens a door and then awaits our response would leave *everybody* outside. This lesser grace is simply not big enough to address our human problem.

Jonah understood God's grace. He knew that God had brought the people of Nineveh to repentance, not through a general offer of salvation but through a specific intervention in their lives. God could easily have left these people under the judgment they so richly deserved. But no! God sent His Word. Even then, when Jonah preached the Word, God could have allowed nature to take its course. Left to themselves, the people of Nineveh would have rejected the Word, and Jonah's preaching would simply have confirmed them in their sin. But no! God's Spirit worked in their hearts, producing repentance and bringing new life.

God was under no obligation to do this. He had done it freely, and that was what was so galling to Jonah. Why would God do such a thing? The more Jonah thought about God's grace, the more angry he became.

Undermining your own repentance

O LORD, is this not what I said when I was still at home? That is why I was so quick to flee to Tarshish. (Jonah 4:2)

If God's grace makes you angry, you need to find out why. For Jonah the answer was simple: he had undermined his own repentance, and it happened while he was at prayer!

Jonah wanted to explain *why* he refused God's call to preach in Nineveh. Reflecting on his experience, Jonah wanted God to know that he had an explanation for his actions, and he felt that there was some justification for what he did. He knew that God was slow to anger. He anticipated God's grace towards the people of Nineveh. That is why he was so quick to flee to Tarshish.

As soon as you start explaining *why* you sinned, you undermine your own repentance. Deep in your soul there is an ongoing struggle between repentance and self-justification. Repentance says: "I did this, and I take responsibility for it. I am sorry, and I ask for your forgiveness." Self-justification says: "You need to understand the reasons *why* I did this. Let me give you an explanation."

Even after you repent of a sin in your life, you may find yourself thinking, "Actually, there's another side to this. Look at the pressure I was under, the difficulties I was facing, the lack of support that I had. It's easy to understand how I fell. In fact it would have been amazing if I hadn't fallen!" Do you see what is happening? You are undermining your own repentance.

A man has an affair. He repents. He takes responsibility and he is truly sorry. But a few weeks later, his tone changes. He begins to explain himself: "Here's *why* it happened," he says, and his explanation undermines his repentance. Eventually he is sure that it was all somebody else's fault. He moves away from repentance and climbs the path of self-justification.

It is possible to undermine your repentance even in the act of making an apology: "I'm sorry I lost my temper, but what *you* said just pushed me over the edge." The explanation kills the apology.

A subtle change had taken place in Jonah's heart. Earlier, he had seen himself as a sinner whose only hope lay in the mercy of God. Now he was in the process of convincing himself that he could explain the wrongs in his life to God. There's all the difference in the world between these two conditions of heart.

In pursuing this path of self-justification, Jonah shifted the blame for his sin onto God, and that was the root of his anger. "I went to Tarshish, and I know that was wrong, but actually, God, it was *Your* fault! If *You* judged the wicked like You should, there wouldn't have been a problem, but I know that you are a God who relents from sending calamity. That is *why* I was so quick to flee to Tarshish."

Explaining sin is big business in America, and the tragedy is that it leads many into the dead end of long-term hostility towards God. The pattern is clear from the experience of Jonah: Explaining sin undermines repentance and undermining repentance leads to anger with God. Thank God it doesn't end there!

You're angry: Let's talk about your rights

Have you any right to be angry? (Jonah 4:4)

It is interesting that when Jonah is angry, God raises the issue of rights. Have you any *right* to be angry? Jonah had a problem with the justice of God; God had a problem with the injustice of Jonah. God had stepped into Jonah's life, in an extraordinary and unparalleled way, with the purpose and effect of saving him. God had been under no obligation to do this. He had acted freely. How many people do you know who have been saved by God sending a great fish to swallow them and bring them safely to dry land?

Jonah's deliverance was the clearest possible example of God doing for one man what He does not do for others.

God had exercised His freedom to shower mercy on Jonah and save him from imminent destruction. And now, God had chosen to show the same mercy to the people of Nineveh. So what was the basis of Jonah's complaint? Do you have any *right* to be angry?

Have you undermined your repentance by offering up explanations of your sin? Do you find yourself blaming God for what has happened in your life? "It's *Your* fault, God ... *You* made me like this... *You* put me in this position." Have you found that the path of self-justification leads to anger against God?

Then listen to God's question: Have you any right to be angry? Recognize that the path of self-justification can only lead you to a dark abyss, and get back to the path of honest confession and repentance as you embrace again the mercy of God in Jesus Christ.

You don't want to spend eternity in the company of those who are angry about God's grace.

Love of a stronger kind

Some people get angry about God's grace, because it seems to make His love less. They feel that a God who says, "Jacob I have loved ... Esau I have hated," seems less loving than a God who would say, "I have loved Jacob and I love Esau too." If God is love, should He not treat all people the same?

No. A love that treats everyone the same is a very weak kind of love.

Let me tell you about a stronger kind of love: I love my wife. That means I treat *nobody* else the same! A good husband does not love all women equally! The strength of his love lies in the fact that it is unique to his wife. His wife feels loved because he has sought her out and he loves her unlike any other. The Bible (in John 3:29) speaks about the love of Christ like this: He has a bride!

The strongest love is not a general benevolence but a passion for the good of a particular person. All of us want to believe that God loves us like that. Those who take a lesser view of grace often try to get there by saying, "If I was the only person in the world, Christ would still have suffered and died for me."

It surprises me how often I hear Christians say this and the degree to which they seem to be helped by it. The statement is a theoretical one, relating to a circumstance which is self-evidently not true. I am *not* the only person in the world.

I'm convinced that the reason some Christians raise this theoretical scenario is that all of us want to know and to feel that we are uniquely loved by God, and a general benevolence in which God opens the door of salvation to all people doesn't feel like God loving me in any direct or personal way. So people who don't believe that God has taken any special initiative to save them resort to saying that if, in theory, nobody else existed, God would still have sent Jesus for them.

Here's the crux of this chapter: I want you see that God *does* love you in a unique and special way. The way you know this is not by speculation over a theoretical scenario in which you might be the only person in the world, but by the glorious reality of His grace intercepting your life, to draw you to faith in Christ. If you are in Christ, God has done more than open the door of salvation for you. He has brought you in! Christ has done more than make your salvation possible. He has saved you.

Can you see how knowing and believing this leads to a deeper experience of God's love? Before you were ever born, God the Father loved you and planned to save you. Christ came into the world for you, and when He died on the cross, He had you in view. You can say with Paul, "The Son of God loved *me* and gave himself for *me*." The reason you can know this with confidence is that the Holy Spirit has brought you to faith and repentance. You did not get there on your own. God saved you! He has taken the initiative, not only by sending His Son into the world, but by breaking into your life, and bringing you to faith and repentance. God was looking for you before you were ever looking for Him. He found you, and that is why you found Him.

My prayer for you as I write this chapter is that your soul will be filled with a new appreciation of the love of God, that you will feel that He loves you more intimately, more personally than you had known before. Once you have a taste of this love, you will spend the rest of your life savoring its richness, and then when your faith is turned to sight, you will know this love in all its fullness, and revel in it forevermore.

Why did God set His love on you? That's a mystery you will never be able to fathom. The nearest we get to an answer in Scripture is that God loves His people ... because He loves them.

The LORD did not set his affection on you and choose you because you were more numerous than other peoples ... But it was because the LORD loved you. (Deut. 7:7-8)

God did not love you because of your background, your intelligence, your good looks, your prayers, your ministry, your commitment, your faith, or your good life. God loves you … because He loves you. Let that lead you to worship.

Finding joy in God's sovereign grace

Christians disagree on how we should understand God's grace, and if you find yourself at odds with the trajectory of this chapter we can agree to differ. That's okay. Your eternal future hangs on your relationship with Christ through faith, not on your understanding of how God's grace and our response relate together in a person's salvation.

Why am I then writing about this? Because I believe that a great deal of your joy in worship *does* hang on this. The more you see of God's grace, the more marvelous and mysterious it will seem to you. And as you are taken up with the wonder of God's redeeming love in your life, you will discover a growing joy in your heart and a deepening desire to pursue a God-centered life.

Take a moment to reflect on God's grace in your life. Think about the friends and members of your family circle who do not love Christ. Some of them have the same background and similar gifts to you. Ask this question: Why is it that you are in Christ and someone else in your family, workplace or group of friends is not? It's not because you're wiser than they are. It's not that you are a better person. And it's not enough to say that you made a better choice. *Why* did you make a better choice?

Here's why you believe: God has set His love on you. God's Holy Spirit awakened you. God drew you to Himself. He redeemed you. He gave you new life from above, and you did nothing to deserve it! That's grace, and it is amazing.

Isaac Watts wrote a hymn in which he takes up our Lord's image of salvation being like a great banquet. Picture yourself coming into a grand banqueting hall where a marvelous feast is spread out for you.

> *While all our hearts and all our songs*
> *Join to admire the feast*
> *Each of us cry, with thankful hearts,*
> *"Lord, why was I a guest?"*

Does this not amaze you? Lord, why me? Why am I in Christ? Why did you bring me in? Why has your grace laid hold of *me*?

> *Why was I made to hear thy voice*
> *And enter while there's room*
> *When thousands make a wretched choice*
> *And rather starve than come?*
>
> *'Twas the same love that spread the feast*
> *That sweetly drew us in;*
> *Else we had still refused to taste*
> *And perished in our sin.*

Apart from God's grace, you would *never* have come to Christ, and neither would I. Our sinful hearts would have taken us away. We would be outside, like thousands of others, still refusing to come.

So let God's grace lead you to worship. Once you taste God's grace, you will spend the rest of your life coming back to this question: 'Why me?' The staggering answer is that He loved you simply because He loved you.

Grace moved John Newton to worship. If you asked him, "What's so amazing about grace, John?" he would say, "I was lost and God found me! I was blind and God healed me! And why God would do this for me, when thousands live their lives and die their deaths still lost and blind is amazing beyond anything I can imagine or begin to explain!"

> *Amazing grace! How sweet the sound*
> *That saved a wretch like me!*
> *I once was lost, but now am found;*
> *Was blind, but now I see.*

The great American theologian, Jonathan Edwards, experienced a wonderful breakthrough in his life in which a fresh understanding of God's grace led him to a new experience of joy and freedom in worship.

For some time, he had struggled with God. Like Jonah, he was offended by grace, and found God's sovereign freedom objectionable. George Marsden describes what happened:

> *While one part of him was powerfully drawn towards full commitment, another part stiffly resisted. ... Since childhood, as he later depicted it, he had been "full of objections against the doctrine of God's sovereignty, in choosing whom he would to eternal life, and rejecting whom he please; leaving them eternally to perish, and be everlastingly tormented in hell. It used to appear like a horrible doctrine to me."*

> *He desperately wanted to trust in God, yet he could not believe in, let alone submit to, such a tyrant.*

> *In the midst of this turmoil, he had a breakthrough. Suddenly he became convinced that indeed God was just in "eternally disposing of men, according to his sovereign pleasure."*

Later, when Edwards was reading the Scriptures, he wrote:

There came into my soul, and was as it were diffused through it, a sense of the glory of the divine being; a new sense, quite different from anything I had ever experienced before. ... I thought ... how happy I should be if I might enjoy that God, and be wrapped up to God in heaven, and be as it were swallowed up in him. [*]

Has something like that happened to you? Have you ever come to a place where God's grace seems gloriously, inexplicably wonderful to you? My prayer for you is that the magnitude of God's grace may grip your heart and lead you to worship. Grasping a compelling, biblical vision of the sovereign grace and goodness of God will lift you out of the shallow water of self-interest and lead you into the pursuit of a God-centered life.

---

[*] George Marsden, Jonathan Edwards: A Life (Yale University Ptress, 2004), pp. 40, 41. Edwards was reading from 1 Timothy 1:17 (KJV), "Now unto the King eternal, immortal, invisible, the only wise God, be honor and glory forever and ever. Amen."

6
Submit to God's Providence

When our family went on vacation to a small cottage in the north of Scotland I was ten years old. The place was so remote that cars were rarely seen, which was great because my brother and I were able to play football on the road until, inevitably, we kicked the ball into a neighboring field.

There's nothing surprising in that, except that the field was a bog. Our ball sat on some tufts of grass ten yards behind the fence, surrounded by a watery marsh. My father decided to retrieve the ball. As he stepped over the fence the moss was solid beneath his feet, but with every step into the field, the ground became less stable. By the time he reached the ball, the field was visibly moving as the thick moss undulated like a water-bed under his weight. My father retrieved the ball and got out, but only just.

Disappointment and confusion over events in your life are like a bog or a quicksand that can quickly pull you under.

Your business fails and you lose the will to begin again. Your children abandon the faith and you wonder if you were a good father or mother. Years pass and you have not yet found the special person you hoped to meet.

Rolling along on the highway of life, you suddenly encounter a bend in the road and you find yourself facing a nightmare for which you were completely unprepared. Plunged into the deep end of pain you now struggle with thoughts you never imagined would enter your mind.

A coldness towards God creeps over your soul. It kills worship, inhibits service, restrains prayer, and silences testimony, leaving you in a joyless relationship with God that resembles a dysfunctional marriage in which people who once loved each other no longer speak.

In this chapter we're going to see how God met with a disappointed believer to deliver him from a life of bitterness and resentment. Jonah's deliverance was *not* immediate. His story ends on a strangely unresolved note and at first sight it seems unfinished. But the writing of the book is the completion of the story. As we have seen, Jonah was moved to write in the form of a confession, in which he tells us more about his struggles than his triumphs, so that we will find hope in our times of greatest darkness.

Jonah will not offer a trite answer to the painful mysteries and disappointments of your life. He never suggests that there is some experience in which your tears of anguish and loss will suddenly be wiped away. In plain and simple language, he tells how God met him in pleasure and in pain, moving him to a place where, instead of indulging his grievance, he could write a confession in which God gets all the glory.

If you feel disappointed with what God has allowed in your life and are jaded by the difficulties you continue to endure, these pages are for you. My prayer, as I write, is that God will meet with you as he met with Jonah, and bring you into a new measure of peace and joy.

The vine, the worm and the wind

"Have you any right to be angry?" … "I do … I am angry enough to die." (Jonah 4:4, 9)

Jonah's anger was not marked by outbursts of rage but by a quiet withdrawal from the company of others and a growing preoccupation with the events of his own life. "Jonah went out and sat down at a place east of the city. There he made himself a shelter, sat in its shade and waited to see what would happen to the city" (Jonah 4:5).

Put yourself in Jonah's shoes. You are on your own, sitting in the desert, just a few miles from a city you really don't like. You are filled with a mixture of anger, resentment, and disappointment. You are not happy about your life.

The sun is beating down on you, and you decide to make a shelter. There isn't much to work with in the desert, just a few stones, some water and clay, enough to make a few mud bricks. You make the best of what you've got, and put up a modest shelter.

The vine

The LORD God provided a vine and made it grow up over Jonah to give shade for his head to ease his discomfort. (Jonah 4:6)

'Miracle-Gro' never produced anything like this! It was a miracle vine. Picture a time-lapse video, showing the growth of a plant from seedling to full maturity in a matter of minutes. That's how this vine appeared. It was a miraculous gift from the Lord. God saw how miserable Jonah was and gave him this gift to ease his discomfort.

"Jonah was very happy about the vine" (v. 6). That's hardly surprising. I can imagine Jonah looking at his baked clay shelter, and then looking at the mass of green foliage on the vine, and saying, "God's shelter is much better than mine."

The vine was God's gift that brought comfort, joy and blessing to Jonah. So what is your vine? What brings you comfort and joy? Where do you see the kindness of God in your life?

The worm

> *At dawn the next day God provided a worm, which chewed the vine so that it withered.* (Jonah 4:7)

When Jonah woke up the next morning, he was anticipating another day of comfort, blessing and joy under God's vine, only to find to his astonishment that the plant had been destroyed as quickly as it had appeared.

Now put yourself in Jonah's shoes: "God, what in the world are You doing? You gave me comfort, blessing and joy through a vine, and then a worm comes and destroys my happiness! One day You pour out Your blessing, the next day You take it away!"

The vine brought comfort, blessing and joy to Jonah. The worm brought him sorrow, disappointment and loss. So what is your worm? What has brought you sorrow? What has God taken away from you? Where have you experienced loss?

The wind

> *When the sun rose, God provided a scorching east wind, and the sun blazed on Jonah's head so that he grew faint.* (Jonah 4:8)

Try to put yourself in Jonah's shoes again: The sand is blowing in your face, and the sun is beating down on your head. Losing the vine was bad enough, but now, on the same day, God seemed to be adding insult to injury by sending the east wind.

The vine brought comfort, blessing and joy. Then the worm brought sorrow, disappointment and loss. Now, the wind brought pain, affliction and distress. So what is your east wind? What aggravates your life? What do you wish would go away?

Is God always in control?

The vine, the worm and the wind: Which of these comes from God?

You might think that God gave the vine, and that He 'allowed' the worm and the wind. But the words of Scripture could not be clearer:

- *God provided* a vine (v. 6).

- *God provided* a worm (v. 7).

- *God provided* a scorching east wind (v. 8).

Jonah wants us to understand that God's hand was as much in the worm and the wind as it was in the vine. That raises some big questions. How can the great sorrow, disappointment and loss of your life come from the hand of God? How can He be present in your pain, affliction and distress?

Before attempting an answer, let's step back and look at the alternative. A colleague told me the story of a couple who endured the tragic loss of their teenage son through a road accident. In their sorrow, they reached out to a pastor who told them, "Sometimes even God makes mistakes." Perhaps the pastor was lost for something to say, but the medicine he offered was worse than the wound he was trying to heal.

A god who bungles the safety of our children is not the sovereign Lord of the Bible. It is better by far to face the dark mysteries of life with your unanswered 'why' than to peer into the abyss of suffering outside of His control and therefore beyond His help.

Most pastors have heroes and role models and one of mine is Alan Redpath. He was the pastor of Moody church in Chicago, and then served in my home church—Charlotte Chapel in Edinburgh, Scotland. Redpath knew about suffering. During his ministry in Edinburgh, a severe stroke threw him into a spiritual crisis, in which he proved the faithfulness of God.

During some difficult years in my own life, I carried his picture in my Bible along with some words he had written from his own experience:

There is no circumstance, no trouble, no testing, that can ever touch me until, first of all, it has gone past God and past Christ, right through to me. If it has come that far, it has come with a great purpose, which I may not understand at the moment. But I refuse to panic, as I lift up my eyes to Him and accept it as a coming from the throne of God for some great purpose of blessing to my own heart.

Alan Redpath knew that God's hand was as much in the wind that brought him pain, affliction and distress and in the worm that brought him sorrow, disappointment and loss as it was in the vine that brought him comfort, blessing and joy. Nothing comes into your life without going through the hand of God first.

The meaning of providence

Providence means that every detail of your life is ordered by the kindness of God who works in all things, the evil and the good, for your ultimate joy. This truth is written all over the Bible, and it is the key to your deliverance from the morbid introspection that ties your heart to the disappointments of life.

When Christ says that your heavenly Father sees a sparrow fall to the ground, He is telling you that God orders the smallest details of life. When He says that the hairs of your head are numbered, He is telling you that God knows you better than you know yourself, and everything about you is important to Him.

The story of Jonah is peppered with testimonies to God's intricate care over every detail of life. Fish swim to God's appointed location. Plants flourish at His word. Worms eat their fill at His command. Ships in the port, storms on the water, and winds in the desert all bear witness to the providence of God.

God 'provided' the great fish by which Jonah's life was spared, and He 'provided' the vine, the worm and the wind to deal with the selfish anger that lurked in Jonah's heart. God's hand is at work in all of the events of your life and there is purpose in all that He does.

The Christian life centers around two amazing gifts that become yours through faith in Jesus Christ: justification and sanctification.

Justification is an event in which God forgives your sins, clothes you in the righteousness of Christ and irrevocably drops all charges against you because, being joined to Christ by faith, all that He has accomplished in His life, death and resurrection is yours.

Sanctification is a process in which God works by His Spirit through the Word to weaken the expressions of sin in your life and to cultivate the fruit of the Spirit so that you will bear an increasing resemblance to His Son, Jesus Christ.

To put it more simply: in justification God forgives you *through* Jesus; in sanctification, God makes you *like* Jesus. God cares about your justification because He does not want you to perish, and He cares about your sanctification because He is not in the business of bringing unchanged rebels into His home.

God's purpose, over time, is to produce an increasing likeness to His only Son in the lives of each of His adopted children. This great and eternal purpose is your highest good and it will be your greatest joy. Nothing else will even come close.

God 'provides' for your sanctification through gifts that bring you joy, disappointments that bring you sorrow, and trials that bring you pain. He uses the vine, the worm and the wind to reproduce the likeness of Christ in you.

It's easy to see how God can use the vine. Every good gift comes from God and when his gifts are rightly received, they lead us to praise and thanksgiving. But how can God use the worm and the wind? How can God's ultimate purpose in your life be advanced by the worm of sorrow, disappointment and loss, or the wind of pain, affliction and distress?

Saved from a vine-centered life

God used the worm and the wind to save Jonah from a vine-centered life. A vine-centered person is one who is so taken up with the joy of God's gifts that he or she ends up loving the gifts more than the Giver.

Jonah had been angry before God gave him the vine, but the vine made him happy. The anger seemed to have gone, but in reality it was only hidden from view. When the vine was destroyed, Jonah's anger resurfaced with a new vigor and a fresh focus.

God said to Jonah, "Do you have a right to be angry about the vine?" "I do," he said. "I am angry enough to die." (Jonah 4:9)

Jonah was trapped in a deep-seated resentment towards God. The vine masked his problem for a time, but when the worm and the wind came, Jonah's heart was exposed and he said that he was angry enough to die. He had found his joy in the vine to such an extent that, when God took it away, he no longer felt that he had a reason to live.

It is possible to love the vine so much that when it withers you wonder if there is any reason left for living. The Bible has a name for this: idolatry. If you feel that without a certain person, or position, or achievement, your life would not be worth living, you may be deeper into idolatry than you think. Friends, family, money, ministry and success are good gifts from God that can bring you great happiness in life. But they are not the purpose of life. Thank God for the vine, but don't live for the vine. The reason to live lies not in the gifts, but in the Giver!

Martyn Lloyd-Jones is another of my preaching heroes. I only heard him speak on a few occasions, but over the last thirty years, his books and recorded sermons have been a constant source of help and inspiration to me. I rarely go through a week without reading something from him.

My friends knew him well and one of them told me that towards the end of his life, one of his colleagues had visited the great man while he was confined at home. "How is it with you, Doctor?" the colleague asked. "You have traveled the world preaching to vast crowds of people. Now you are confined to this room. How are you doing with this?"

Lloyd-Jones replied with the words of Jesus:

> *Do not rejoice that the spirits submit to you, but rejoice that your names are written in heaven.* (Luke 10:20)

Lloyd-Jones had enjoyed the vine of God's blessing on his ministry, but he did not live for the vine. The vine will pass away; God's love for you will never pass away. So find your greatest joy, not in the vine but in knowing that you belong to Christ.

Job's vine, worm and wind

Jonah was not alone in experiencing the joy of the vine, the loss of the worm, and the pain of the wind. Job experienced the same pattern of God's providence, but he responded in a very different way. Putting these two stories together will help you to see the divergent paths from which you must choose when God allows you to experience the vine, the worm and the wind in your life.

Think about Job's vine: He had one wife, seven sons, and three daughters. Besides that he had 7,000 sheep, 3,000 camels, 500 yoke of oxen, 500 donkeys and a large number of servants. This man had a strong family, a thriving business and great wealth. The Bible says, "He was the greatest man among all the people of the East" (Job 1:3). That's some vine!

Then God sent the worm. Disaster struck. In a single day Job's financial security, represented by his animals, was completely wiped out. His servants were killed in violent terrorist attacks and, worst of all, the house where Job's children were enjoying a party collapsed on them. No one survived. That's some worm.

Then God sent the east wind. Job's wife, to whom he might have looked for support, said to him, "Curse God and die!" (Job 2:9). At this point, Job's health broke down, and painful sores broke out over his body. Then his friends arrived and, instead of bringing comfort, their trite religion only increased this poor man's affliction (Job 2:11).

Job and Jonah responded in very different ways to the vine, the worm and the wind in their lives. Jonah was angry enough to die. Job fell to the ground in worship and said, "The LORD gave and the LORD has taken away; may the name of the LORD be praised" (Job 1:21).

It is often said that Job is a book about suffering. That's true, but there's something deeper going on. The key question in this story is not, "Why do good people suffer?" but "Why would anyone love God?"

The world and the devil assume that the only reason anyone would love God is pure self-interest. This was Satan's point at the beginning of the story. His hatred for God is so deep that he cannot believe anyone would love God for who He is. So the devil asked this question: "Does Job fear God for nothing?" (Job 1:9). Satan assumes that Job loves God simply because He has showered him with good gifts: family, wealth and stature. What more could a man want? Of course a man will love the God who gives him all these things. But what if God takes them away?

So the great drama rolls out. Job's vine was chewed by the worm, and it disappeared in a single day. Then the east wind began to blow. Would Job fear God and love Him still in the face of this unexplained suffering? Or would he follow the advice of his wife, and the impulse of Jonah, to end his life and give up on God? The honor of God's name was on the line. And it is on the line in your journey through pain and suffering today.

Whatever work you do for the Lord, it may be that the greatest contribution you will make to the advance of Christ's kingdom is to love Him still through pain and suffering. I often say this to people who are battling their way through great sorrow and disappointment. Usually they are surprised. But it's true. By loving Christ still in pain that is hard to bear and in mysteries you may never understand, you contribute to the advance of Christ's kingdom in more ways than you know. Cynics are unsettled, believers are strengthened, heaven rejoices, and hell shudders in consternation.

Job went through a thousand agonies in his sorrow, but the worm and the wind were his finest hour. In his pain he worshiped, and there is no higher worship than that which comes out of your pain and your loss.

Confessing faith with unanswered questions

Some years ago, when Karen and I were visiting with her family in England, all of the talk was about her youngest sister's baby that was due to be born in a few weeks. We were on the beach when a phone call came saying that Kathy was in great pain. Her placenta had split, and Kathy was rushed into hospital, for an emergency delivery of her baby.

Megan was put on a ventilator as soon as she was born. After four weeks, she was making little progress and so was air lifted to a specialist unit in Southampton, where she was given open-heart surgery.

Two months later she had a further procedure to open the aorta tube entering her heart. The process failed and so they tried it again. When it failed a second time they had to resort to further surgery. Throughout this time, Megan gained very little weight and continued to be dependent on the ventilator. By the grace of God she survived, but this was only the beginning of a long journey.

When Megan reached her first birthday, she was still not able to sit, and when her parents asked the specialist if their daughter would walk, the specialist declined to answer.

After that year of trauma, and all kinds of unresolved questions, Wayne and Kathy planned a service of dedication to coincide with their daughter's first birthday. They were part of a small congregation who surrounded them with love and prayer. On this day, attendance at the church was doubled as the various branches of my wife's family gathered for this special occasion.

The highlight of the service came when Wayne and Kathy spoke. Kathy described how their faith had been tested. Then Wayne got up and thanked everyone who had supported them. "Right now," he said, "we don't know what the future holds for Megan. I have all kinds of unanswered questions about life. And still have some desperate low points. But I believe in God. And I believe that Jesus Christ is the Son of God and that He died for me." It was one of the finest confessions of faith I have ever heard.

Sometimes, we confess that Jesus is Lord with raised hands and joyful hearts. At other times, we confess Him through gritted teeth and with many tears. In the course of a lifetime God will give you the opportunity to glorify Him both ways.

Moving away from resentment
Every person is on a journey leading in one of two directions: either we are loving God more or we are resenting God more. When Christ winds up human history, there will be two great gatherings of people: One will worship God forever; the other will hate Him forever. Every person is moving along one of two lines, either to perpetual joy in God, or perpetual resentment towards God. Every day we are moving nearer to heaven or to hell.

We saw in the last chapter that God's grace will make you angry or it will lead you to worship. The same is true of God's providence. The vine, the worm and the wind will make you angry or they will lead you to worship. So how can you move away from resentment towards God? How can you learn to love God more than you love His gifts?

Growth in the Christian life flows from a communion with Christ in which you love Him by savoring the depth of His love for you. "We love because he first loved us" (1 John 4:19). The more you see God's love for you, the more you will grow in loving Him.

This is why Paul prayed so passionately that Christian believers would know more of the depth and length and breadth of Christ's love. You will grow in love for Christ as you get a clearer view of His love for you. So think about the vine, the worm and the wind in the life of our Lord Jesus. What was the vine that brought Him comfort, blessing and joy?

He chose twelve disciples and called them to be with Him. They were his friends and he found joy in their companionship (Mark 3:14). Through their ministry He saw Satan fall like lightening, and on their return, His heart was filled with joy through the Holy Spirit (Luke 10:18, 21).

Then the worm came. The disciples, who had brought Him comfort, joy and blessing, all forsook him and fled. Judas betrayed Him with a kiss. Peter denied him with a curse, and Jesus was plunged into sorrow and loss.

And then the east wind blew. Not only did the disciples desert Him, but he was scourged, mocked and crowned with thorns. He was nailed to the cross, plunged into darkness and, in His affliction, He cried out to His Father, "My God, my God, why have You forsaken me?" (Mark 15:34). Why was this happening to *Him*?

Christ endured the worm and the wind so you could be brought into an eternity under God's vine.

As you think about the unanswered questions of your life, think about the great unanswered question that rose from the darkness and agony of your Savior's suffering: "My God, *why*?" There was no answer to that question. The heavens remained dark and silent as Christ suffered.

But in the darkness, and through the unanswered *why*, Christ loved and trusted the Father still. When it was fin-

ished he said, "Into your hands I commit my spirit," and
that splintered the gates of hell.

John Newton's surprising answer to prayer

John Newton wrote a hymn that describes how God repro-
duces the likeness of Christ in the lives of His children.
These words came out of Newton's experience and I quote
them here, not only because they are so insightful, but also
because Newton used the story of Jonah's vine to describe
what happened in his own life.

> *I asked the Lord that I might grow*
> *In faith, and love, and every grace;*
> *Might more of his salvation know,*
> *And seek, more earnestly, his face. …*
>
> *I hoped that in some favored hour,*
> *At once he'd answer my request;*
> *And by His love's constraining power,*
> *Subdue my sins, and give me rest.*

I'm with Newton here, and I expect you are too. I would
really like God to give me victory over all temptations and
rest from all my troubles. But Newton found that God
answered his prayer for growth in a different way:

> *Instead of this, he made me feel*
> *The hidden evils of my heart;*
> *And let the angry powers of hell*
> *Assault my soul in every part.*
>
> *Yea more, with his own hand he seemed*
> *Intent to aggravate my woe;*
> *Crossed all the fair designs I schemed,*
> *Blasted my gourds, and laid me low.*

The vine in Jonah's story was referred to as a 'gourd' in the King James Bible that Newton would have used. God blasted his gourds! I love that phrase, but I don't like the reality that it represents. God blasted away the sources of comfort and joy in John Newton's life. He sent the worm and the wind to this man who had been praying for growth in faith and love!

> *"Lord, why is this?" I trembling cried,*
> *"Wilt Thou pursue Thy worm to death?"*
> *"Tis in this way," the Lord replied,*
> *"I answer prayer for grace and faith.*
>
> *"These inward trials I employ,*
> *From self, and pride, to set thee free;*
> *And break thy schemes of earthly joy,*
> *That thou may'st seek thy all in Me."* *

Three simple prayers

There are three simple prayers that you can use on your journey from a vine-centered to a God-centered life. They will help you to appreciate God's gifts and submit to His providence as you tear down the idols that lurk in your heart.

"Lord, help me to receive Your gifts gratefully"

Every good gift comes from the Lord, so as God gives you friends, a job, money, family, or any other gift that brings you comfort, blessing and joy, receive it from His hand with thanksgiving and let it be a source of praise.

---

* John Newton, *Olney Hymns,* 1779.

"Lord, help me to hold Your gifts lightly"

God's gifts are gifts; they are not rights. Confusing gifts with rights opens the door to bitterness and resentment. Gifts come from God. The Lord gives, the Lord takes away, and nothing in this life or in this world lasts forever. So hold the gifts that He gives you lightly. The gifts will pass; the Giver remains.

"Lord, help me to love You more than I love Your gifts"

You do not want to spend your life as an idolater, so aim to take down the idols not by loving God's gifts less but by loving Christ more. And grow in love for Christ by savoring His amazing love for you.

7

Reflect God's Compassion

The greatest challenge I face as a pastor is to wean Christians off a self-absorbed faith that views God as a resource to be drawn on in the pursuit of a picture-perfect life for 'me and my family.' Navigating a God-centered life means getting beyond that kind of infantile faith and developing a passion that reflects the heart of God.

I say this gently because I see the roots of self-absorption in my own heart. Learning to love is a life-long journey, but God cares about lost people, and pursuing a God-centered life will lead you to share His passion.

Across this country, there are millions of people who have no living faith in Jesus Christ. Many of them were brought up in church. They may believe that Jesus died and rose, but it has made little or no difference to their lives. Some of them have been alienated from the church. They think they have tried Christianity and it has failed, but the truth is that they have not yet tasted the grace and love of Jesus Christ.

Some of them have experienced a harsh form of Christianity that majors on demands: "This is what you *need* to do. This is what you *ought* to be." It feels like being hit over the head with a two-by-four, and it leaves many people feeling exhausted and condemned. But Jesus does not drive us by law; He draws us with love. He said, "I, when I am lifted up from the earth, will draw all men to myself" (John 12:32). "All men" does not mean "every single person" but rather, "people from every background." God's compassion does not stop with your family, your church or your nation. The story of Jonah is about God's passion for the world.

God cared about Nineveh and was actively engaged in redeeming thousands of its people through a staggering initiative of mercy and grace. But Jonah had left the city. He was on his own; withdrawn, self-absorbed, introspective and angry. His thoughts were taken up with his own life, and especially with the mystery of why God would have given him a vine and then taken it away.

Do you see this dramatic contrast between the heart of God and the heart of Jonah? God is redeeming sinners as His Spirit sweeps through Nineveh. Jonah is outside the city, absorbed with his own problems and brooding over his disappointments. Compassion was drowning in a sea of self-pity.

So God speaks, shining a light into the prophet's darkness:

You have been concerned about this vine ... Should I not be concerned about that great city? (Jonah 4:10, 11)

The point here is not that Jonah was wrong to be concerned about the vine. As we saw in the last chapter, the vine was a good gift from God; it brought comfort, blessing and joy, and it was to be received, like all of God's gifts, with thanksgiving. The problem was that Jonah's concern for himself had drowned his compassion for others. Consumed by the unexplained mysteries of his own life, he had no room for concern over the unresolved destinies of others. Absorbed in his questions about the vine, he was strangely unmoved by the plight of thousands facing eternity with the worm and the wind.

It is possible to be genuinely grateful for your own salvation, and yet strangely disinterested in the salvation of others. This enigma shaped a large part of Jonah's life, and his book is a candid confession of the contradictions in his own heart and the bitter fruit that came from his self-centered brand of faith.

Jonah believed that God is sovereign and yet tried to run from Him. He received God's grace in his own life and yet was reluctant to share it with others. He saw God at work in miraculous ways and yet found no joy in what God was doing. This was the path that led Jonah to sit alone in a desert, angry with God and despairing of himself. Jonah was concerned about the vine while God was concerned about the city.

I recently got into conversation with a college student who said that he had been brought up in church but had rejected Christianity. I asked him why. "I've come to the conclusion," he said, "that it's just too selfish to be true." The Christians he had known had been absorbed in themselves. The church where they worshiped was about meeting the needs of its own members. The God they worshiped existed to make them healthy, wealthy, and happy.

The salvation they believed in was about making sure that they didn't go to hell, but the plight of others wasn't on their radar screen.

Self-absorbed Christianity is an oxymoron. As you set your sail to navigate a God-centered life, you will grow in compassion that reflects the heart of God.

The staggering value of a single life

Nineveh has more than a hundred and twenty thousand people ... Should I not be concerned about that great city? (Jonah 4:11)

The place to begin is with the value God places on every human life. The life of one person is worth more than the entire assets of the whole world. This is implied in our Lord's question, "What good is it for a man to gain the whole world, yet forfeit his soul?" (Mark 8:36). Think about that: One soul is of greater value than the whole world. The world and everything in it will pass away. A human life is forever, and that gives it greater value than the whole world.

Every person you meet is a unique creation of God with a particular calling in life and an eternal future of indescribable happiness or unfathomable loss. In the words of C. S Lewis,

The dullest and most uninteresting person you can talk to may one day be a creature, which if you saw it now, you would be strongly tempted to worship, or else a horror and a corruption such as you now meet, if at all, only in a nightmare. ... There are no ordinary people. You have never talked to a mere mortal. ... It is immortals whom we joke with, work with, marry, snub, and exploit—immortal horrors or everlasting splendours. *

---

* C. S. Lewis, *The weight of glory, and other addresses* (Macmillan, 1980), pp. 18–19.

When you sit next to someone on a train, or stand in line at the grocery store, remind yourself that God made this person. There is no one else quite like this person anywhere in the world, there never has been, and there never will be again. God cares about this person and right now, He has placed you next to them, so you should care about them too.

Take an interest in people, and you will grow in compassion. If, like me, God has made you with a more introverted personality, you won't find this easy. But I find that the ability to take an interest in people lies more in the condition of my heart than in the cast of my temperament.

I've also found that taking an active interest in others is healthy for my own soul. A wise pastor gave me this great advice: "Irrigate your soul in the joys and sorrows of other people." It works. When your soul is dry, and it feels like the weight of the world is on your shoulders, find a way to reach out to someone in obvious need, and you will be helped.

Compassion is easy if you allow yourself the luxury of choosing the people for whom you will care. But God's glory is seen in the scope of His compassion: "The LORD is good to *all;* he has compassion on *all* he has made" (Ps. 145:9). That doesn't mean that God will *save* all people, but it does mean that He *cares* about all people.

God cares about His enemies, as well as His friends. He loves his enemies and *does good* to those who hate Him: "He causes his sun to rise on the evil and the good, and sends rain on the righteous and the unrighteous" (Matt. 5:45). God gives life and breath to all people. Some use that breath to praise Him; others use it to curse Him. God sustains his enemies even while they are sinning against Him. The breath that they use to rage against God is sustained by Him, even while they are raging!

Reflecting on this amazing kindness of God will help you to grow in compassion, especially for people whose beliefs and behavior may offend or repulse you. When you show compassion, you reflect the heart of God.

Hard truths can produce tender hearts

"Nineveh has more than a hundred and twenty thousand people who cannot tell their right hand from their left ... Should I not be concerned about that great city?" (Jonah 4:11)

God's concern for the people was related to the fact that they could not tell their right hand from their left. What does that mean? It could be that the 120,000 people who could not tell their right hand from their left is a reference to young children, but I think it is much more likely to be a description of people who have lost their moral compass, and are no longer able to discern between good and evil.

We use 'right' and 'left' to give directions: "Go down the street and take the third turning on the *left*, then take the fourth on the *right*. The house is half way down on the *left* side of the road." A person who cannot tell their right hand from their left will soon lose their way and become hopelessly lost.

God says, "I have compassion for Nineveh because it is a city of 120,000 lost people. They cannot distinguish good from evil. They are in complete moral confusion, and for that reason I have compassion on them." It's worth pausing to take this in. God has compassion for these people precisely *because* they cannot distinguish right from wrong. His compassion is drawn out by their moral bankruptcy.

You might think that words like moral confusion and bankruptcy seem a long way from the world of compassion, but I want to show you that this need not be the case. A robust and biblical doctrine of sin, properly applied, will help you to grow in compassion. So let's look at what that means and how it works.

The Bible describes our fallen human condition in many ways, but three words will get us to the heart of the problem: Blindness, slavery and death.

Blindness

The god of this age has blinded the minds of unbelievers, so that they cannot see the light of the gospel of the glory of Christ, who is the image of God. (2 Cor. 4:4)

Blindness is not a refusal to see; it is an *inability* to see. There's a big difference. As I write, I think about a friend whose daughter broke his heart through her rebellion. Along with his pain, he also experienced frustration and sometimes anger. How could she do these things?

He told me that this verse had helped him. "Her blindness is real," he said. "She doesn't see the glory of Christ, and it's not just that she doesn't want to see—she really *can't* see, and nobody gets angry with a person who is blind for their inability to see." Grasping his daughter's spiritual condition helped my friend to deal with his frustration and grow in compassion.

Reflecting on the human condition will help you to grow in patience and it will enlarge your heart to reflect the heart of God. It will make you more caring and less condemning; less like Jonah, and more like Jesus. Remember that the blindness of your unbelieving friends or loved ones is real. When you talk to them about Christ, they don't get it. They *cannot* see. And that's only the beginning of the problem.

Slavery

I tell you the truth, everyone who sins is a slave to sin. (John 8:34)

Being a slave to sin means that the sinner can't stop sinning. He may want to stop, but he does not have the power to do so. He may be able to change the particular form of his sins, but he cannot stop being a sinner. That's what slavery means, and the slavery is as real as the blindness. But the effects of sin on the human soul go deeper still.

Death

As for you, you were dead in your transgressions and sins. (Eph. 2:1)

Being dead in sin means that by nature we are unresponsive to God. A corpse does not have the power to change its own position. It cannot act and it cannot move. This is why Jesus said, "No one can come to me unless the Father who sent me draws him" (John 6:44).

The human condition is that, spiritually, we are all born blind, bound, and dead. This biblical teaching about sin, *improperly* applied can lead to harshness, condemnation and a sense of human worthlessness. That is how it was with Jonah. He despised the evil people of Nineveh, and felt that they deserved destruction. His doctrine of sin eroded compassion.

But God also saw the evil of Nineveh, and He had compassion on the people precisely because they did not know their right hand from their left. Grasping the effect of sin on the human soul can help you grow in compassion that reflects the heart of God. A simple illustration will show how this works.

Imagine for a moment that you are responsible for parking at the Super Bowl. The cars are jammed in, bumper-to-bumper, and when the game ends, your job is to clear the parking lot as quickly and as safely as possible. The job carries some authority, so you are given a uniform, a flag and a whistle.

Your strategy is simple. As soon as the drivers in the first row of a section arrive at their cars, you begin moving them out into the exit lane so that others parked behind them can follow. After the game, a flood of people make their way to the parking lot. You notice three drivers, seated in their cars in the front row of one section, so you raise your flag and wave them forward.

Nothing happens. You blow the whistle. You point to them and wave the flag again, but still nothing happens. Then you notice something strange—these guys are in their cars, but they haven't even started their engines. What in the world are they doing?

By now, the folks in the cars behind are wondering the same thing. Some of them are sounding their horns. People are getting frustrated. Why are the guys at the front not moving?

You start getting angry yourself. It's your job to clear the parking lot and these guys are holding you and everyone else back. So you walk over to the cars. That takes time and leads to even more blaring of horns. Some people are rolling down their windows and shouting abuse at the drivers on the front row.

You get to the first car, and bang on the windshield: "Get moving!" The driver rolls down the window. "I don't know what happened," he says, "but I can't see. I got in the car, and everything went dark. I can't drive. I'm blind!"

You go quickly to the next car, and bang on the windshield: The second driver tries to roll down his window, but has great difficulty. You look at his wrists and you see that he is in handcuffs. "I don't know how this happened," he said, "but I got in the car and some guy was hiding in the back seat. He slapped these handcuffs on me and then took off. I can't drive, I'm bound!"

By now, the folks in the cars behind are getting ready to riot: Horns are blaring and people ten rows back are standing on pick-up trucks, waving their fists and shouting abuse.

You move to the third car, and bang on the window. "Sir, these guys have a problem. They can't move their vehicles. I need you to move your car now!" There is no response. You look more closely. The driver in the third car is slumped over the wheel. He is dead.

Picture the scene: Crowds of people are shouting abuse, blaring their horns, and bellowing what they will do to the drivers in the front row, if they don't get moving. Everyone is angry, but you have compassion. Why? Because you understand the problem; one man is blind, another guy is bound and a third is dead.

There is a kind of Christianity that is angry with the sinful world, and it is reflected in a brand of preaching that rails against the evils of our time. It is angry because it really does not adequately reflect on the human condition: By nature, we are blind, bound and dead. We *cannot* see the glory of Christ, we *do not* have the power to stop sinning, and we *will not* come to Christ and follow Him.

Blaring the horns of condemnation may give vent to Christian frustrations but it will do nothing to solve the problem. Hope lies not in shouting commands from a distance, but in the power of a new life that is the gift of God in Jesus Christ. Grasping this gospel principle will help you to grow in compassion.

Reflecting the compassion of Jesus

People become like the gods that they worship. Whatever you admire you will in some measure reflect. This simple truth is a warning against idolatry. The idols of the nations have eyes but they cannot see; they have ears but they cannot hear. "Those who make them will be like them and so will all who trust in them" (Ps. 115:8). The principle is clear: When people worship idols that cannot see or hear, the capacity of their souls to see and hear will be diminished. The nations become like the gods they worship.

For the Christian, the same principle opens up wonderful horizons of hope. As we *behold* the glory of the Lord, we are transformed into His likeness with ever increasing glory (2 Cor. 3:18). Again, the principle is simple: you reflect what you see. Glory will be reflected in you, *as you see Christ's glory*. Holiness will deepen in you as you see His holiness. It follows then that compassion will grow in you *as you see His compassion*.

I find that I need to be intentional about seeing God's compassion. His holiness, righteousness and judgment come to my mind more easily. I picture Him in unapproachable light. I have to cultivate the wonderful truth that He draws near in unfathomable love. I am helped when I read, "As a father has compassion on his children, so the Lord has compassion on those who fear him; *for he knows how we are formed*" (Ps. 103:13-14).

God has compassion for you because He knows how you are formed. He knows what you are made of, and He knows this, not only because He is your Creator but, because in Jesus Christ, God has assumed human form and lived our human life from the inside.

Christ knows more about your life than any pastor, counselor or friend ever could. He knows this from His own experience.

- Are you exhausted? Jesus has been there. He fell asleep in a boat. When your strength is gone you can come to Him; He knows what it is like.

- Do you have loved ones who are deeply resistant to Christ? Jesus has been there. His own brothers said that He was out of his mind.

- Do you live with the tension of disloyalty on your team? Jesus has been there. Judas was one of the twelve, but he had his own agenda. Jesus knew the full horror of treachery from his own inner circle.

- Are you moved by the plight of people living without hope in the world? Jesus is with you. He saw crowds of people like sheep without a shepherd and He had compassion on them.

- Do you feel angry about injustice and abuse in this world? Jesus would say, "Me too!" He was furious over the self-interest of temple rulers who had excluded foreigners from their place of worship by turning the court of the gentiles into a market.

- Are you grieving the loss of someone you love? Jesus has been there. He has felt the gut-wrenching pain of weeping by a graveside. He knows what that is like.

- Does the future seem so dark that you can hardly bear to think about it? Jesus has been there. When He came to the Garden of Gethsemane, He was overwhelmed with sorrow.

- Have you suffered injustice? Jesus has been there. Read the story of Holy Week.

- Have you ever felt without hope, without help, without comfort and without God? Jesus has been there. Nailed to a cross, alone in the darkness, all awareness of the loving presence of His Father was taken from Him at precisely the moment when he needed it most.

Try to take in the staggering reality of God the Son entering life as you know it. You will feel His compassion and, as you do, you will feel that you can come to Him (Heb. 4:15-16).

The greatest compassion this world has ever seen came from the cross, where Jesus prayed for those who had caused

His suffering: "Father, forgive them, they do not know what they are doing" (Luke 23:34). His compassion flowed from His perfect knowledge of the human condition. "They do not know what they are doing." This blindness does not remove our responsibility. Our guilt is real. That's why Jesus prayed for forgiveness. But Christ sees more than our guilt. He also sees the blindness, slavery and death that lies behind it, and that is why the redeeming work of Christ is *more than* forgiveness. Christ gives sight to the blind; the Lord sets prisoners free; God raises us to new life in Christ.

Think about someone who annoys you, a person who really gets under your skin. You know that you need to grow in compassion for them, but it isn't easy. Reflect on the human condition in relation to that person—he or she is blind and bound and dead. Think about that. It will help you to grow in compassion.

But what if the person who irritates you most is a Christian? The same principle applies. One reason why difficult relationships between Christians cause so much anxiety is that we feel we should be able to resolve problems between brothers and sisters in Christ. Often we do, but it is not always possible. That is why Paul says, "*If it is possible, as far is it depends on you, live at peace with everyone*" (Rom. 12:18).

If the person who causes you distress is a believer, remember that, while God has given him sight, he only sees in part (1 Cor. 13:12). While God has given her His Spirit, she still battles with the flesh. Though every Christian is a new creation in Christ, no Christian is yet what he or she will be. Every Christian is a work in progress. Reflect on all this and you will grow in compassion.

The jaded preacher and the new believer

The strategies we have considered for growing in compassion have been rooted in the mind. As God's Word reshapes your convictions, God's Spirit will renew your feelings. You will grow in reflecting God's compassion as you press forward in your pursuit of a God-centered life.

Grasping how change happens in the Christian life is of huge importance and, once you see it, you will find that the grand market of Christian techniques, secrets and disciplines for changing your life loses the appeal it might once have had. It's like drinking a good cup of coffee and then wondering why you settled for what you had before.

Transformation begins with the renewing of your mind, but it does not end there. Compassion involves action, engagement and commitment. It's more than a feeling. It is love in action.

Look at what God *did* out of compassion for Nineveh:

- He called Jonah and sent him;

- He sent a storm to intercept Jonah;

- He exposed Jonah's sin;

- He prepared a great fish to save Jonah;

- He caused the fish to spew Jonah onto the beach;

- He called Jonah a second time;

- He revealed the message that Jonah was to preach;

- He gave faith and repentance to the people;

- He changed the heart of the king;

- He poured out a spirit of prayer among the people;

- He relented from sending disaster.

Compassion is more than feeling sorry for people in their lost condition. It is taking action so that redeeming love may reach them.

The final scene in Jonah's story involves two contrasting pictures that need to be viewed together. The prophet is alone, isolated in the desert, consumed with his own interests, taken up with the disappointments of his life. Meanwhile, back in the city, God's Spirit is at work as a great revival is sweeping through Nineveh.

People were coming to repentance and faith, and when the King of Nineveh heard God's Word, "he rose from his throne, took off his royal robes, covered himself with sackcloth and sat down in the dust" (Jonah 3:6). The king sat down in prayer and repentance (that's the significance of the sackcloth) and called on the people to do the same. "Let everyone call urgently on God. Let them give up their evil ways and their violence. Who knows? God may yet relent and with compassion turn from his fierce anger" (Jonah 3:8-9).

The contrast is striking. The king is in the city, actively engaged in praying for the salvation of his people. As a new believer he is already reflecting the heart of God. But Jonah the prophet is outside, absorbed with his own problems, watching to see what will happen.

In every church there are people who are working and people who are watching. Some, like the king, extend themselves in the hope of making a difference. Others, like the prophet, indulge their private arguments with God and position themselves as observers while the eternal future of thousands hangs in the balance. Hearts grow cold on the sidelines of ministry, so follow the example of the king—get involved in what God is doing and you will grow in compassion.

Compassion is more than pity expressed from afar, more than taking a distant interest in how events will unfold. In his first hours as a new believer, the king got down in the dirt and made intercession for his people. He reflected the heart of God which the prophet, with his lifetime of ministry experience, was yet to discover.

The Savior, the monk and the beggar

The story is told of a monk who had given himself to prayer. All his life he had longed that, just once, Christ would appear to him in his cell. He had prayed this for years and then one day it happened.

The monk had been praying and, as he looked up, there *He* was: The Lord Jesus Christ was standing right in his cell! The monk was completely overcome. This was the moment he had longed for all his life. An audience with Jesus Christ! His mind was filled with a thousand questions he wanted to ask. The moment he had longed for all his life had finally arrived.

At that moment, the bell over the door of the monastery rang. The monk knew what that meant. Each day, a beggar would climb the hill to the monastery and ask for bread. That day, the monk was on duty. It was his job to open the door.

The monk was faced with an agonizing decision. Should he leave the Savior and feed the beggar, or stay with the Savior knowing that the beggar would come back another day?

The monk made his decision. Slowly, and with great reluctance, he left his light-filled cell, opened the monastery door and gave the beggar some bread. Then, with great sadness, the monk walked back to his room, distraught that serving the beggar had cost him the moment of a lifetime.

When the monk returned to his cell, to his absolute astonishment he found that the Savior was still there, waiting for him to return. The monk fell to his knees in wonder, and the Savior said to him, "If you had not gone, I would not have stayed."

Compassion means sharing a 'common passion' with God. It means caring about lost people as God does, and getting involved in His mission in the world. Begin by reflecting on the unique value of every person you meet, and by remembering the blindness, slavery and death that plague the human condition. But don't stop with these convictions and the feelings of compassion that will flow from them. Move into action. Get engaged in ministry. Start praying for lost people.

Be like the king, not like the prophet. Choose the company of those who are working, rather than the comfort of those who are watching. You will grow in compassion and it will become obvious that you are pursuing a God-centered life.

8
Rejoice in God's Salvation

Interventions happen when people have lost the ability to help themselves and those who love them are unwilling to stand by and witness their self- destruction. Sometimes people can so lose touch with reality that they no longer see the damage they are doing to themselves and even if they did, they do not have the ability to change.

Interventions are always painful, both for the person who suddenly has to face the gruesome reality he fought hard to avoid, and for the loved ones who know that the person in need has neither the will nor the power to change the path he has chosen. Sometimes a person's desire is so destructive that it would be callous to leave her to her own choices. An intervention is the only hope.

In these pages, we have followed the story of God's dramatic interventions in Jonah's life. It is a story full of hope, reminding us of what God can do, not only for those who seek Him but also for those who, like Jonah, have determined to shut Him out.

Some Christians see God as a kindly but passive observer of our choices. After all, God wouldn't ever interfere with our free will, would He?

Ask Jonah and a wry smile would come over his face.

★ ★ ★ ★ ★ ★ ★

Would God ever interfere with our free will?

Hmmm ... let's see.

I had made my choice. I suppressed my conscience, steeled my nerves and, by a free act of my own will, boarded the ship to Tarshish. But God would not let me go.

My will was taking me in the wrong direction. So God made an intervention, graciously messing with my rebellious heart to save me from a life wasted in disobedience.

God stepped into my life uninvited, through an unexpected storm, rolling dice, and pounding waves that pushed me down until, finally, I came to my senses and called on the Lord, only to find that He had already planned and provided for my salvation by sending a great fish.

But that was only the beginning. Having stretched myself out in ministry, I experienced a strange darkness in which I was overcome by resentment. Left to myself, I would have slouched into retirement angry with God and bitter about the events that had shaped my life. But God stepped in and showed me His compassion.

Would God interfere with our free will? I'm glad He interfered with mine! Left to myself, I would still be running from God, and who knows where I would be today? Rebellion and resentment were my foolish choice. Salvation comes from the Lord.

★ ★ ★ ★ ★ ★ ★

Jesus told a parable about a prodigal son and an elder brother. Jonah was both. Like the prodigal, he ran in open rebellion against God. Like the elder brother, he served the Father but festered in hidden resentment. God's intervention brought a double deliverance, and the ultimate triumph of God's grace in Jonah's life is reflected in his writing a book where God gets all the glory.

It is a mark of Jonah's humility that a man who was so remarkably used by God gave us this honest confession of what was happening in his inner life. Jonah takes no credit for the transformation in his life or for the powerful effect of his ministry. He confesses his own self-centeredness both before and after his preaching to Nineveh, and leaves us marvelling at the grace of God who would not let his servant go.

As we have traced Jonah's journey we have picked up the paths to a God-centered life. Jonah was transformed by a compelling vision of God: His sovereign power, His endless patience, His relentless love, and His triumphant grace. In this final chapter, I want to show you how God-centered convictions about your salvation will help you navigate a God-centered life.

Salvation that brings a lasting change

Salvation comes from the LORD. (Jonah 2:9)

These words fly like a banner over Jonah's story, communicating his life message in a single sound bite. But what do they mean?

'Salvation' is a word that has been cheapened in our time. The evangelist invites people to come raise their hand or make a decision so that they can be 'saved.' Mr and Mrs

Jones are sitting together listening to the preacher. Mrs Jones goes to the front at the invitation, says the prayer and she is told that she is saved. But Mr Jones is not convinced. He does not go forward and, in the months that follow, his scepticism is increased because, while his wife is now sure she is saved, he cannot see any difference in her life.

Mrs Jones has a rather sharp tongue and an appetite for gossip and, when she gets going, people say they wish she was more like Mr Jones, who really is a very kind man! Any reasonable person would say, "This doesn't make sense. Something is missing!"

Something *is* missing. Mr and Mrs Jones have been presented with a truncated version of the gospel, in which a person can make a decision that changes their future destiny without changing their present life.

If you have struggled with that kind of emaciated Christianity, you will be glad to discover that salvation is more than saying a prayer or making a decision. It is a completed transaction, a continuing process and a future outcome, all of which come from the Lord.

Justification: A completed transaction

Your salvation is a completed transaction. "It is by grace that you *have been saved*" (Eph. 2:8). Notice the past tense. Christ died for your sins and rose for your justification (Rom. 4:25). When you are made one with Christ through the bond of faith, God counts all your sin as if it were Christ's and all Christ's righteousness as if it were yours. The completed transaction of your salvation is called justification. This amazing gift comes from the Lord, and it means that your salvation is a done deal.

Sanctification: A continuing process

But your salvation is also a continuing process. "The message of the cross is foolishness to those who are perishing, but to us who *are being saved* it is the power of God" (1 Cor. 1:18). Notice the present tense. You are a new person in Christ but you are not yet what you will be (1 John 3:2). Your salvation has begun but it is not yet complete. You are fully forgiven but not yet fully restored. You still struggle with the flesh and you fail in many ways. But God has not abandoned you to defeat. You *are being saved,* and the continuing process of your salvation comes from the Lord.

This process of salvation is especially clear in the story of Jonah. As a prophet, Jonah had known and served the Lord for many years. But his own heart still misled him. Even at the end of the story when Jonah became angry and frustrated, God was still saving this mature believer from the treason in his own heart. I'm so glad that the story of Jonah does not have a 'happy ending' in which all of Jonah's struggles are resolved.

The process of straightening out what is twisted in you continues *throughout your life* and will only be complete when you arrive in heaven. Until then, you are in the process of waging war against sin as God forms the fruit of the Spirit in you. Waging war and growing fruit both take time. Salvation is a lifelong process in which God is always working to make you more like Jesus. This continuing process is called sanctification, and it comes from the Lord.

Glorification: A future outcome

Your salvation is also a future outcome. Peter speaks about "the salvation that is *ready to be revealed in the last time*" (1 Peter 1:5). The Lord will bring this future salvation when

He takes you into the presence of God (1 Thess. 4:16-17). The glory that will be revealed in you then will make the trials of your life now seem very small (Rom. 8:18). *God will wipe all tears from your eyes, and Christ will lead you into all the joys of eternal life* (Rev. 21:3-5).

Your salvation has begun in the completed transaction of justification. It continues in the ongoing process of sanctification. It will be completed in a future outcome that the Bible calls glorification. And all of this comes from the Lord.

The work of a good shepherd

Jesus told a marvellous story about a good shepherd who had a flock of a hundred sheep (Luke 15:1-7). One of them was lost, and so the shepherd went out to find it. When the sheep was found, he put it on his shoulders and brought it back to the fold.

A shepherd who opened the gate but then left the lost sheep to find their own way home would have an empty fold. The lost sheep do not know where the fold is. The open gate is of no use to them. They are lost and they cannot find it! The lost sheep need a good shepherd who will search for them, find them and carry them home on His shoulders. Jesus is the good shepherd. He does more than make salvation possible. He saves!

I had been a pastor for several years before I grasped that salvation comes from the Lord. For many years I believed that God opens the door of salvation and then stands back, leaving it up to us to decide if we want to come in. Then, over time, I began to see that God has done more for me than make my salvation possible. He saved me.

Grasping this marvellous truth has been life-changing for me. It has deepened my worship, strengthened my assurance, motivated me in prayer and evangelism, and helped me in counselling parents in distress.

Knowing that salvation comes from the Lord helps me in navigating a God-centered life. If God had made my salvation possible, and then stepped back, refusing to interfere with my 'free will', the entire Christian life would be about me—my believing, my serving, my following, my choices to live a good Christian life.

But seeing that God has come after me and laid hold of me and brought me to His fold has opened up for me a new sense of worship and wonder, a new awareness of His love, and a new confidence in what God can do in the lives of others.

"Salvation comes from the Lord"

The central message of this book is that God-centered convictions, clearly grasped and properly applied, will help you to navigate a God-centered life. Here are some ways in which you can use the great truth that "Salvation comes from the Lord."

1. Deepening your worship

Thousands of kids grow up believing that Christianity is all about them making the right choices: Going to church, reading the Bible, saying their prayers, believing in Jesus, taking a step of commitment, saying 'no' to sex, drink, drugs and pornography, hanging out with good people, and thanking God that He made it all possible.

That's light years from the world of the Bible. It is a salvation that comes from your self, made possible by the Lord. What is there in this that would lead you to worship?

God does more than make salvation possible. He saves. His love is seen not only in sending His Son into the world, but in breaking into the lives of particular individuals to save them. Jonah knew this from his own experience. He saw that God was actively involved in all the events of his life, working for his ultimate good, and this led him to worship:

> *You* hurled me into the deep,
>   into the very heart of the seas,
>   and the currents swirled about me;
> all *your* waves and breakers
>   swept over me.
> I said, "I have been banished
>   from *your* sight;
> yet I will look again
>   toward *your* holy temple."
> To the roots of the mountains I sank down;
>   the earth beneath barred me in forever.
> But *you* brought my life up from the pit,
>   O Lord my God.
> When my life was ebbing away,
>   I remembered *you*, Lord,
> and my prayer rose to *you*,
>   to *your* holy temple."
> Those who cling to worthless idols
>   forfeit the grace that could be theirs.
> But I, with a song of thanksgiving,
>   will sacrifice to *you*.
> What I have vowed I will make good.
>   *Salvation comes from the Lord.*
>   (Jonah 2:3-9)

You can't get more God-centered than that! Jonah is full of praise. He lifts up His heart to God and says, "Lord, you are the One who saves! It's all *You*! I was done for, sinking down in the ocean, without help or hope, and *You* saved me!

Think about what God has done in your salvation. Take a look at what lies behind your faith in Christ. See what God has done and your heart will be warmed in worship.

God set His love on you before you were born. All your days were written in His book before one of them came to be (Ps. 139:16). Before the creation of the world you were on God's horizon, and he planned all your days in love (Eph. 1:4). When Jesus came into the world, He came to save real people with names and faces and if you are in Christ you are among them. The sins he carried were your sins. The hell he endured was your hell.

God did all of this for you before you were born, but it didn't end there. He brought His salvation to you, opening your eyes to see your sin, and drawing your heart to find hope in the Savior. Every Christian has a unique story of how this took place. The times, the places and the people involved vary, but behind each story, however simple, is an same amazing miracle of God's grace.

My story is the simplest of all. In May of 1964, I heard a children's talk in our home church in Edinburgh. The pastor said that being in a Christian family does not make you a Christian. Each of us needs a personal faith in Christ. God used his words to speak to my heart and the following morning, with my father's help, I invited Christ into my life and trusted Him as my Savior. I was six years old.

Looking back I marvel at what God was doing. Behind the simple act of a small boy opening his heart to Jesus, the Father was at work drawing me to Christ through the faithful words of a pastor. Imagine the scene in heaven as God sends His Spirit.

> *"Go work in that little boy's heart. Speak to him, draw him to Christ. Give him life from above. Direct his life. Call him. Equip him. Guard him. Keep him. Stay with him. Correct him (he'll need that). Strengthen him. Show him the truth. Help him to pray. And bring him safely home to Me."*

The more I think about the mystery of God's saving work in my life, the more staggering it gets. Seeing that your salvation comes from the Lord will deepen your worship. It will take you beyond a system of propositions to be believed, and bring you before the Lord in wonder at His mystery and of His grace in your life.

2. Praying for your unconverted friends and loved ones

The most frequent objection to an emphasis on salvation coming from the Lord is that this might inhibit evangelism and diminish prayer. It's easy to understand this fear. If salvation comes from the Lord, won't that lead to Christians sitting back and waiting for God to do His work? Believing that salvation comes from the Lord, in fact, has had the opposite effect in my life. This belief has sustained me in prayer and motivated me in evangelism.

Think about people you love who right now are far from God. They are not Christians and they are not interested in becoming Christians. If their salvation depended on their will, you would be no hope for them, for the obvious reason that *their will is already clear.* They have made their choice and, like Jonah, they are heading in the wrong direction.

But if God is free to swoop down, uninvited, and lay hold of a person who is spiritually dead, and bring them to spiritual life, you have reason for hope! If God saves people who are not looking to be saved, you can ask *Him* to save them. I can't imagine a more powerful incentive to pray.

Hope comes not from a 'hands off' God who stands back and observes our decisions but from a 'hands on' God who is able and willing to step into our misdirected lives, and turn us around so that we begin to love what we used to hate and hate what we used to love.

Some parents live under the intolerable burden of believing that the salvation of their children is up to them. This leads to two temptations. One is that if your children become godly men and women, you may be tempted to take the credit. The other is that if your children turn away, you be tempted to take the blame.

In a culture with multiple seminars and programs on how to raise your children, the idea can get around that if we just get this parenting business *right*, our children will be followers of Christ. Over the years I have met many parents who beat themselves up, taking the blame for their children being on the wrong path. "I didn't pray enough. I didn't teach enough. I didn't spend enough time. I blew it. If only I had done a better job."

I've also met a few parents who seem to have taken the credit. One couple, with two daughters who were following the Lord, spoke to me about their friends whose daughters had sadly turned away from Christ. The parents of the Christian girls had been scrupulous in their discipline of family prayers and felt that their friends should have followed their example. "If only they had done what we did, it would all have been so different," they said; and in saying this they robbed God of all the glory for the salvation of their children.

Salvation comes from the Lord, not from you. If your children believe, let God have the glory for their salvation. If they do not believe, trust them to Him, look to Him and roll the burden onto His shoulders, knowing that He hears your prayers and He cares for you.

The God who sends storms, worms and winds is free to make an intervention at any time and in any way in the life of any person, and that includes the friends and loved ones for whom He invites you to pray.

So come to God and ask him to sweep into the closed mind, the hard heart and the rebellious will of your loved one who has no interest in coming to Christ. Tell the Lord that he does not need their permission. Appeal to Him as the God who says, "I revealed myself to those who did not ask for me; I was found by those who did not seek me. To a nation that did not call on my name, I said, 'Here am I, Here am I'" (Isa. 65:1). Tell Him that they cannot save themselves and that if He leaves them to their own choices, they will be lost forever. Plead with the Lord to exercise His freedom and glorify His name in saving them.

3. Sustaining your commitment to evangelistic ministry
Knowing that salvation comes from the Lord is a powerful incentive in the work of evangelism. God saves through the gospel. Faith comes by hearing, and hearing by the Word

of God (Rom. 10:17). Knowing that God swoops down into people's lives *through the gospel* motivates me in making the gospel known. Who knows what God will do through your witness to Christ?

The first disciples made their living from fishing and Jesus said to them, "I will make you fishers of men" (Mark 1:17). Think about this picture. These men were skilled in throwing out the net and drawing in fish. But how would that work with *people*? The disciples would throw out the net of the gospel. They would speak about Christ. But people are not like fish. How many unbelieving people want to be caught in the gospel net?

Our Lord spoke the words of life as no one else could, but most of his audience were supremely disinterested in what He said. After offering the finest teaching this world has ever heard, Jesus said, "You have seen me and *still you do not believe*" (John 6:36). Where do you go from there?

That question is of huge importance for everyone who engages seriously in serving the Lord. You set out to reach people with the gospel, and you engage in some ministry for this purpose. But the people you are trying to reach show little interest in the gospel. After a while you get discouraged and feel like packing it in. What's the point? Is it really worth it?

How do you keep going? What will sustain you in gospel ministry when many do not believe? I have found great help and encouragement from the words of Jesus when He was faced with precisely this situation:

Problem: *"You have seen me and still you do not believe"* (John 6:36).

Answer: *"All that the Father gives me will come to me"* (John 6:37).

Faced with the overwhelming unbelief and disinterest of his audience, Jesus found strength in the great truth that salvation comes from the Lord. The Father gives people to His Son. These people will come to Him, and nothing can stop them.

How will they come? Jesus says, "No one can come to me unless the Father who sent me draws him" (John 6:44). The Father gives people to Christ; He is actively engaged in drawing them. The result of this is that they come. Not just some of them, but all of them. "*All* that the Father gives me will come to me." We get used to working in percentages. How many contacts turn into sales? How many students end up graduating? How many airplanes arrive on time?

The answer is always a fraction of the whole. But if we ask how many of the people given by the Father to the Son come to Him, the answer is 100 per cent. And Jesus says, "I shall lose none of all that He has given me, but raise them up at the last day."

What if the Father had not given people to the Son? What if He was not actively engaged in drawing them? How many would come then? Left to ourselves, nobody would ever come! The work of evangelism would be impossible. Far from being a hindrance to evangelism, knowing that "salvation comes from the Lord," properly understood and applied, is the greatest possible incentive for sharing the gospel.

The apostle Paul experienced the practical encouragement of this wonderful truth when he faced great opposition to his evangelistic ministry. He had arrived at Corinth, the Las Vegas of the early world, and gave himself to preaching that Jesus is the Christ. But he was up against a hostile audience. The people of the synagogue where he was preaching became abusive, so he left and started meeting in the home of a man called Titius Justus.

Then one night, Christ spoke to Paul in a vision:

Do not be afraid; keep on speaking, do not be silent.

For I am with you, and no one is going to attack and harm you, because I have many people in this city (Acts 18:9-10).

Since there were only a few believers in the city at the time, the 'many people' were those who would come to faith in the future. The risen Christ knew who they were. The Father had given them to Him and, through the Spirit, He would draw them to faith through Paul's courageous ministry.

I can't imagine a greater motivation for sustaining the work of evangelism than to know that:

1. In every place Christ has people who have been given to Him by the Father.

2. The Father will draw them through the gospel, and

3. When He does, they will come to Christ.

There are people around you who will come to Christ. You don't know who they are. You don't need to. Your work is to share the gospel. God's work is to draw sinners to Christ, and when He draws them, they will come. So speak about Christ with confidence. God is always at work.

Don't ever worry about whether a person to whom you are speaking is one of those given by the Father to the Son.

The truth of the Father giving people to the Son is there to encourage you and sustain you in sharing the gospel with others. The invitation you are to make, and the promise you can give is, in the words of Jesus, "Whoever comes to me I will never drive away" (John 6:37).

We are to invite people to come to Christ indiscriminately. When Jesus says that whoever comes to him He will never drive away, He makes an open invitation to all people, and we must do the same.

I recently had a fascinating conversation with a high school student who told me that for some years he had been worried about whether he was one of the elect. I don't know many high school students who have worried about that, but it had been a problem to him. So I asked him how he had resolved the problem. "I realized," he said, "that if I do not come to Christ I would never know. So I came to Christ and now what used to worry me has become a great joy."

4. Renewing your strength in the battle against sin
Christian believers are in a strange position. Every part of your soul has been made new, but no part of your soul is wholly or completely new. Think about an old house that is being renovated. Work has begun in every room, but there is no room in which the renovation is finished. Nothing in the house is as it was, and nothing in the house is as it will be. The work continues and life goes on in the house until it is complete.

If you have lived through a major home remodeling, you will know how difficult that is, and that's why this is a helpful picture of the Christian life. Salvation, as we saw, is a continuing process. You are not what you were and you are not what you will be. That is why you experience continuing struggles against sin that remains in your mind, your heart and your will throughout the course of your life.

I've been drawn to the story of Jonah because it is the story of a mature believer, widely appreciated for his ministry, who was still struggling with the treachery of his own heart. Jonah extended himself in ministry and in the process discovered hidden layers of self-interest in his soul. Sinclair Ferguson describes this as 'the missionary experience':

> *Taken out of his normal home context, working under pressures never before encountered, sensing the frustration of a new culture and language so different from his own—these can bring the very worst out of a person, and often do. Sensitivities appear that are hitherto unknown, or could be hidden in our Christian fellowship at home. The bold knight errant who rides into foreign parts with high aspirations and expectations of fervent evangelism, of a ministry teaching the indigenous church, may soon find out that God has removed him across the face of the earth more for the sake of his own sanctification than that of others! There he may find what a narrow minded, prejudiced, conceited, prayerless, fruitless and uncooperative believer he really is in his heart of hearts; as a missionary once shared with me, "I never knew what a heart of stone and filth I had until I went overseas."* *

Where can you go when you discover the treachery of your own heart?

Jesus says, "Come to me, all you who are weary and burdened, and I will give you rest" (Matt. 11:28). You have done your best to live a godly life, but you feel crushed by the inadequacy of your own attempt to please God. You

---

* Sinclair Ferguson, *Man Overboard* (Pickering and Inglis, 1981), p. 86f.

have become weary and burdened by the sheer pressure of trying to live up to a standard of godliness and you are exhausted by it. You are doing your best, but your life is a relentless treadmill and you are weary.

I am so glad that Jesus does not say, "Practice more spiritual disciplines." He says, "*Come to me* ... and I will give you rest." How will Christ give you rest? He says "Take my yoke upon you ... and you will find rest for your souls" (Matt. 11:29). The yoke does not sound like good news, but it is. The yoke was a wooden beam that tied two animals together so that they walked and worked in tandem. To be yoked to Christ means that the Son of God pulls your load with you.

Being yoked to Christ will get you through. The load you could not pull alone with Him is bearable. The battle you could not fight alone with Him is winnable. You are not on your own in the struggle. The Son of God is for you. He stands with you. And He is in you. Salvation comes from the Lord.

5. Settling your assurance of arriving in heaven

Knowing that your salvation comes from the Lord will help you to enjoy a settled confidence about your final arrival in heaven. If your entrance through the pearly gates depended on your commitment to follow Christ, how do you know that you could keep it up? The best you could do is to say, "I'll give it my best shot, and I hope that I make it."

I was moved by a conversation I had with a Christian lady, in which she told me that for years she had worried what would happen if she were to suffer from Alzheimer's disease. "If I had Alzheimer's," she said, "I might not have the presence of mind to believe in Christ when I die. What would happen to me then?"

Thank God we are not saved by the strength of our faith but by the strength of our Savior. Salvation comes from the Lord, not from your faith. Christ saves you. Faith means that you trust Him to do it. Assurance about your ultimate arrival in heaven will be strengthened, not by looking at your performance in the Christian life but at the Savior, who died and lives to bring you there.

On the night before His suffering and death on the cross, Jesus prayed for His disciples and for all believers. Try to picture this: the Son of God, on His knees, praying for you. Having prayed for His disciples, Jesus says, "I pray … for those who will believe in me through their message" (John 17:20). If you believe the gospel and have trusted your life to Christ, this prayer is for you.

Jesus says, "Father, I want those you have given me to be with me" (John 17:24). Think about this: The Son of God says to the Father that He wants you in heaven. A wise person writes a will before he dies and Christ, knowing that He is approaching death, announces His will to the Father. In just a few hours, He will wear the crown of thorns. Nails will be driven into His hands and His feet. If you ask Him, "Jesus, what do you want to come from this?" He would say, "I want those the Father has given me to be with me." Your first assurance of heaven is that Christ wants you there. The Christ who died to save you lives to keep you, and He will bring you home. Salvation comes from the Lord.

But Christ adds something else in His prayer:

Father, I want those you have given me … to see my glory, the glory you have given me because you loved me before the creation of the world (John 17:24).

Christ wants you to see His glory. And He tells you why this must happen: The Father loves the Son, and out of this love glorifies Him as the God-man for all eternity. God created the world as a theatre in which His Son's glory would shine. He permitted the catastrophe of sin because a redeemed creation will reveal Christ's glory more than an innocent one ever could.

Read the book of Revelation, where God reveals the splendors of heaven. Picture the angels and the vast company of the redeemed from every tribe and nation and ask, "Who is all this *for?* Why are all these people here?"

You will be in heaven for the glory of the Son of God who redeemed you, and for the pleasure of the Savior who loves you. Your salvation comes from the Lord. Christ gets what He wants, and His declared will is that you should be with Him and that you should see His glory. There can be no higher assurance than that.

JOSEPH
The Hidden Hand of God
Liam Goligher
ISBN 978-1-84550-368-0

DANIEL
Trusting the True Hero
Sean Michael Lucas
ISBN 978-1-84550-732-9

Christian Focus Publications

publishes books for all ages

Our mission statement –

STAYING FAITHFUL

In dependence upon God we seek to impact the world through literature faithful to His infallible Word, the Bible. Our aim is to ensure that the LORD Jesus Christ is presented as the only hope to obtain forgiveness of sin, live a useful life and look forward to heaven with Him.

REACHING OUT

Christ's last command requires us to reach out to our world with His gospel. We seek to help fulfil that by publishing books that point people towards Jesus and help them develop a Christ-like maturity. We aim to equip all levels of readers for life, work, ministry and mission.

Books in our adult range are published in three imprints.

Christian Focus contains popular works including biographies, commentaries, basic doctrine and Christian living. Our children's books are also published in this imprint.

Mentor focuses on books written at a level suitable for Bible College and seminary students, pastors, and other serious readers. The imprint includes commentaries, doctrinal studies, examination of current issues and church history.

Christian Heritage contains classic writings from the past.

Christian Focus Publications, Ltd
Geanies House, Fearn, Ross-shire,
IV20 1TW, Scotland, United Kingdom
www.christianfocus.com